THE FLYING SCOTSMAN

The Flying Scotsman

Sally Magnusson

Quartet Books
New York Melbourne London

Published in the USA by
Quartet Books Inc., 1981
A member of the Namara Group
360 Park Avenue South, Suite 1300
New York, NY 10010

ISBN 0 7043 3379 1

Manufactured in the USA by
Whitehall Company, Wheeling, Illinois

For Siggy

Acknowledgements

I should like to thank all those who have helped me in so many ways with this book: Eric Liddell's widow and friends, for giving so generously of their time; Stan Greenberg, for checking the passages about Eric's career in athletics, and Twentieth Century-Fox and BBC Radio Scotland for their generous co-operation. But most of all, I want to thank my sister, Margaret Magnusson, who helped me as interviewer, researcher, critic and typist. This book is half hers.

Contents

Introduction

Late in the searingly hot afternoon of Friday, 11 July 1924, Eric Liddell, a twenty-two-year-old science student from Edinburgh University, won a gold medal in the 400 metres at the Olympic Games in Paris. It was a spectacular race, and produced a world record. But there were other people who triumphed spectacularly at those Games: Harold Abrahams of England, who became the first Briton to win the 100 metres; Douglas Lowe of England, who won the gold in the 800 metres; American Johnny Weissmuller, who took three golds in the swimming; and the incomparable Finn, Paavo Nurmi, who won another four in the track events.

Why, then, was it Eric Liddell who was fêted and hero-worshipped for the rest of his life? – who had a fan club dedicated to him, a Scout Patrol named after him, a strip cartoon in his honour in a boys' comic? Why is it Eric Liddell who, nearly forty years after his death, has inspired a film – with Abrahams as his foil – about his part in these remarkable Olympic Games in Paris in 1924?

The answer, of course, is because he refused to run on a Sunday. He captured the imagination of millions by tossing away his chance of a gold medal in the 100 metres – the race he was favourite to win – because a principle of his Christian faith mattered more. When he unexpectedly won the 400 metres instead, the country was at his feet. When he stepped quietly out of the limelight a year later to serve as a missionary in China, Scotland's capital gave him the kind of send-off no departing missionary has received before or since. When he died in a Japanese internment camp, after living away from Britain almost continuously for twenty years, the public reaction was as warm as if he had only left the day before.

Who was this man, Eric Liddell? What kind of person was it who could compete so effectively, yet turn down the chance of Olympic glory so effortlessly . . . who could shrug off all the super-star adulation and head for China as casually as if he were popping off for a week-end in London . . . above all, who had such a shattering impact on all who met him that nobody, nobody at all, ever had a bad word to say of him? For children and adults alike adored Eric Liddell. Even now, those who remember him have only extravagant praise: they call him 'saintly', 'kind', 'loving', 'deeply spiritual'. When he was at the peak of his athletics career, ministers wrote sermons about the goodness of his life, comparing him to Christ. When he died, all Scotland mourned.

Now the 1980s have produced their own act of worship, in the shape of a film. But, surprisingly, it isn't the 'warts and all' debunking of the myth you would expect from our tight-lipped generation towards a Victorian-style, muscular Christian hero like Liddell. David Puttnam, the man who made the world-weary *Midnight Express*, has produced an unembarrassed celebration of the athlete and missionary, called *Chariots of Fire*, arguing that people are hungry for heroism again. Eric Liddell certainly fits the bill: a man who led a simple, spiritual life, turning his back on the rewards of his Olympic fame to disappear into an obscure missionary station.

But conspicuous goodness tends to bother our sceptical generation, and I started the search for Eric Liddell a little warily. There was surely a pair of clay feet there to be revealed; a few weaknesses to be exposed; perhaps, in such a strong-minded man, a streak of spiritual pride, a 'holier-than-thou' attitude. 'But was he really that good?' I would ask people. The answer was invariably the same – sometimes apologetic, sometimes pained, sometimes indignant, but always the same: Yes, he was.

I thought I had found something when I happened on a disillusioning eyewitness account of the behaviour of some of the missionaries in the Japanese internment camp where Liddell spent the last months of his life. I read of tempers lost and heavy moralizing, of exclusiveness and selfishness. The author scarcely had a good word for anyone, but least of all for the Protestant Christians. Then I turned a page and found this:

It is rare indeed when anyone has the good fortune to meet a saint, but he comes as close to it as anyone I have ever known.

Of course, he was talking about Eric Liddell.

I turned, with the deepest gratitude, to the only full-length study of Eric Liddell, a book called *Scotland's Greatest Athlete* by the late Rev. Dr D. P. Thomson (The Research Unit, Crieff, Perthshire, 1970). Anyone who knows the book will recognize the debt I owe to this meticulously researched biography, with its wealth of information elicited from people all over the world. But D. P. Thomson, that veteran war-horse of Scottish evangelism, was an old friend of Liddell's; he is not always the most detached of commentators (although, by the end of my own research, I was beginning to wonder if anyone could be). The film-makers of *Chariots of Fire* found it necessary to invent dissension and to colour the truth to give the sporting part of Liddell's life the interest of some internal and external conflict. But I realized in the end that the way to make Liddell's life interesting was just to tell his story the way it was. His life *was* interesting.

As I spoke to more and more of the people who remembered Eric Liddell, I was struck by the consistency of his life. The old university friend was saying the same sort of thing as the matron who worked with him in a Chinese country mission in the midst of the Sino-Japanese war; the officer with the pipe-band who played at the Paris Olympics was offering the same kind of insights as the schoolgirl from the Japanese internment camp; even the star-struck teenage founder of his fan-club back in the

1920s was saying basically the same thing as his widow in the 1980s.

What was astonishing at first, until it became so usual that I accepted it as a matter of course, was the reception I got from all those I interviewed. Not only was everyone delighted to talk about Eric Liddell, but there was a stream of instantaneous recollections down the telephone at the first contact. It tells you something about Liddell, when you can phone a retired soldier of eighty-seven, hurl a question at him about a man he had not seen for nearly sixty years, and receive a warm, clear and illuminating account of the chats he and Eric had in a hotel lounge during the Paris Olympics in 1924. Or when you can phone a former ship's engineer, who knew Eric in China, with a general question about 'What was Eric like?' – and receive within a few days an unsolicited account of every detail he remembered about him.

The people I met were all like that: quick to respond with anecdotes, anxious to communicate Eric Liddell's effect on them. At first I was almost overcome by the sheer weight of tributes. But gradually it dawned upon me that the very fulsomeness of the praise *was* the story. People were not just being kind about a departed friend. The translucence of memory was not enough to explain fully, although it could in part, the sparkle he seemed to have left behind him. The story was right there – in the impact of his personality. Undeniable, yet a little mysterious, because he seemed so ordinary.

Each day brought a fresh nugget. There was Mrs Elsa Watson, who as a fourteen-year-old schoolgirl had started the Eric Liddell Fan Club, whose teenage members were instructed to live upright lives and 'always to uphold Eric Liddell'. Still as enthusiastic today as she was nearly sixty years ago, and only a touch less ardent, she evoked a glorious picture of her version of 1920s 'Beatle-mania'. Through her we learned, for instance, that residents in a douce block of Edinburgh flats were astonished to look out of their windows one morning in 1924 and observe a strange pattern of Virginia stock and nasturtiums sprouting in the garden below. When they looked closely they could make out the letters 'E.H.L.'. This planting of seeds in the form of her hero's initials was only the latest in a series of acts of worship by young Elsa, which included hoarding the tea-leaves from his empty cup, sending him Valentines (which he answered), following him to athletics meetings and keeping the fan-club members in line.

Then there was Bob Knight, the retired ship's engineer, who insisted in his slow Tyneside way that we get rid of any idea that Liddell was excessively pious, and produced a whole stream of anecdotes – like the time when Liddell non-plussed a group of earnest inquirers about the spiritual quality of his running, by informing them with a grin: 'I don't like to be beaten.'

There was his sister, Mrs Jenny Somerville, the only surviving member of Liddell's childhood family, who could tell us all about the parents who started the tradition of Chinese missionary service and remembered the tiniest details of life in a Chinese village at the turn of the twentieth century.

Miss Annie Buchan, from Peterhead, was another one: a diminutive, white-haired octogenarian, who could recall the details of life in the Chinese country mission where Liddell worked in the 1930s, with amazing clarity. She was matron of the hospital in the same mission compound, she was an inmate of the same internment camp, she was at Liddell's bedside when he died – and all her stories she tells the same way. She tells them simply, clearly, with an eye (after all these years) for the colour of the sky and the expression on Liddell's face when he finds a dreadfully injured man whose head the Japanese hadn't quite managed to chop off.

Professor Neil Campbell, Liddell's fellow student athlete; Mrs Isobel Herron, the schoolgirl in the internment camp who has never forgotten Liddell tearing up his wife's sheets to mend her hockey stick; Tom Riddell, the veteran sportsman who wishes Liddell were around today; General Sir Philip Christison, the officer in charge of the pipe-band of the Cameron Highlanders at the Paris Olympics: there were so many, and their memories not only shed light on Eric Liddell, but opened a fascinating vista on to the social history of the times – on Scotland and China, on war and temperance, athletics and evangelism.

I left his widow until last. By that time I was so curious, so mesmerized by the same charisma that had captivated everyone else, that I approached her with almost childish excitement. You can tell a lot about a man from his choice of wife. And there she was, laughing and vivacious, telling me: 'I can't *stand* these people who are so goody-goody and holy-holy. They bring out the worst in me and make me want to go the opposite way. Eric was never like that.'

She told me about Eric's covert but highly inventive style of courtship, his poker-faced sense of humour, his keenly felt hurt at being called a traitor when he refused to run in the Olympics on a Sunday, his ability to charm exactly what he wanted out of anybody, their home life, their children, the disruptions of living in a country during Japanese occupation. She told me, too, that Ian Charleson in the Twentieth Century-Fox film about Liddell and Harold Abrahams, *Chariots of Fire*, portrayed Eric exactly as she knew him.

Ian Charleson himself proved another source of enlightenment. I will never forget his description of how difficult it was to imitate Liddell's style of running – all arms and legs and head thrown wildly back – and then the sudden flash of insight that had shown him why Liddell ran like that: 'He ran with faith. He didn't even look where he was going.' That was it. Of course, that was it.

What *was* this faith of his, so rooted in what some might call an out-of-fashion religious tradition, yet so potent? What was the source of the serenity everyone talked about? What about his charisma as a public speaker, when everyone said he was such a poor orator? What about his running – was that really 'an emanation of his well-known spiritual fervour', as one commentator wrote?

I was tempted to conclude that there were just unknowable depths to the man, that this was a case of 'simple truth miscalled simplicity'. But 'unknowable' was too easy; we are always so quick to dismiss lives like his as bland, or irrelevant. And I needed to know how it was that Eric Liddell had been able to maintain his spiritual serenity while being obviously so driven to achieve, first in athletics to Olympic standard, then preaching the gospel and working amid the poverty and the horrors of war in a primitive Chinese village, and finally touching all kinds of sordidness in the Japanese internment camp where he died in 1945.

The question of what the 1980s would make of Eric Liddell led me on to another: what would Eric Liddell make of the 1980s? Could he ever have become a world record-breaker today and still have fulfilled the commitments to his faith and the sharing of it that were so important to him? Would there have been the same joy in running, the same throwing back of the head in the sheer exultation of the race, if he had had to submit to the rigours and the professionalism and the extraordinarily exacting standards of sport today? More to the point, could he ever have got away with the quiet announcement of his refusal to run on a Sunday that so impressed his peers, or the uncomplicated decision to slip away from stardom to be a missionary on the other side of the world?

The enigmatic quality of the man would be cornered, the unknowable depths that intrigued people would be superficially plumbed, and once everything had been aired and exclaimed over and explained away, he would be forgotten. He would become ordinary again. And Eric Liddell *was* ordinary, on the surface. He was a very attractive, very conscientious man with a self-sacrificial faith; but there have been thousands of people like that, and there must be thousands more the world over, quietly living good lives and making the same kind of sacrifices without anybody ever hearing about them. And the first to remind us of that would be Eric Liddell – who would curl up with embarrassment at the very idea of being the subject of this book.

1

'His Heid's No' Back Yet!'

The young man who was carried shoulder-high through the streets of Edinburgh after his graduation, just a week after winning a gold medal at the 1924 Olympics, had a wreath of olive leaves on his head, a grin all over his face, and a dimple right in the middle of his chin.

The crowds who lined the pavements as he was borne past that day on a sedan-chair would have noticed, too, that he had rather special eyes. Blue eyes that *twinkled* – there was no other word for it. It was as if he were looking all the time at someone he cared for rather a lot.

At the age of twenty-two Eric Liddell's fair hair was already receding, a state of affairs that his disappointed mother ascribed to too many hot showers after training. His build was slight and wiry, and his walk, people soon remarked, was what could only be described as springy. The less charitable called it bandy-legged.

In looks he took after his father, the Rev. James Dunlop Liddell, an erect Victorian figure with a long face and a luxuriant dark moustache. James Liddell came from the village of Drymen near the southern end of Loch Lomond. He had started his working life as an apprentice in the drapery business in the ancient royal burgh of Stirling, the 'Gateway to the Highlands' as it has been called. But drapery was not to be his metier. In the seaside holiday resort of Helensburgh on the coast of the lower Clyde he met the Rev. William Blair, a minister of the Scottish Congregational Church, who fired him with a different vocation: from then on he wanted only to be a missionary in foreign fields.

In 1893, at a Sunday school picnic in Stirling, he met the girl who was to become his wife. Her name was Mary Reddin – a quiet, gentle girl who wore her dark brown hair up in a bun as was the fashion of those days. She had been born in Paxton in Berwickshire, and was working as a trained nurse in Glasgow; she was now convalescing with friends in Stirling after an illness. They were both twenty-two years old, and got engaged soon afterwards.

Their marriage was not to take place for another six years, however. James Dunlop Liddell went on a course at a Congregational college in Glasgow in order to be ordained, while Mary carried on with her nursing. In 1898 he applied to the London Missionary Society and was accepted for a posting to their mission station in Mongolia, in northern China.

Liddell had wanted to get married first and take his bride out with him. But the London Missionary Society was too canny for that. How were they to know if this ex-draper from Drymen would make the grade in the demanding conditions of the field in a totally alien and even hostile country in the Far East? First he had to go out and prove himself, and pass his exams in Chinese, and only then would they send Mary Reddin out to marry him.

While he was away, Mary Reddin took a job in Stornoway, the capital town of the Isle of Lewis in the Outer Hebrides, looking after the fisher girls who flocked to work there during the summer. Stornoway was then the centre of the great West Coast herring-fishing industry, and the quaysides were alive with activity as the girls plied their sharp knives on the silver catches from more than 300 fishing boats. Accidents were inevitable, and frequent, and Mary Reddin had plenty to do. Her experience of 'instant first-aid' in Stornoway was to stand her in good stead in the paddy-fields of China.

Meanwhile, the Rev. James Dunlop Liddell was working with a will at learning Chinese, and passed his exams in record time. He was a warm-hearted, peace-loving man who quarrelled with no one and was greatly liked by the Chinese and Europeans alike. The London Missionary Society was delighted with him; his posting was confirmed, and after receiving an exultant telegram from her fiancé, Mary Reddin set sail to join him. They married in Shanghai Cathedral on 23 October 1899.

It was not a propitious time for foreigners to get married in China – and especially foreign missionaries. China was seething with unrest and resentment against the foreign Great Powers who had humiliated and degraded her for decades. The disgraceful Opium Wars in the middle of the nineteenth century, whereby Britain (with armed help from France) forced the Chinese to legalize the import of opium against their will, rankled deeply. China's defeat at the hands of Japan in the Sino-Japanese War of 1894–5 was fresh and bitter in the memory. Politically, the Great Powers – Britain, France, Germany, Russia and Japan – seemed intent on dismembering China in their greedy pursuit of land concessions, mining rights and ever-increasing trade monopolies.

Under the circumstances it was not surprising that extreme xenophobia should flourish in China at the end of the nineteenth century. When the Liddells got married in Shanghai in 1899, this hatred of all foreigners was coming to the boil through a secret society called the Yi Ho Chuan, the 'League of Righteous and Harmonious Fists', better known in the West as the 'Boxers'.

For years the Boxers had been openly calling on the peasantry to join a patriotic militia dedicated to the extermination of all foreigners – especially Christian foreigners. The Boxers were fanatics, which made them all the more alarming; and they harboured the bizarre notion of themselves being invulnerable to bullets.

In June 1900, the Boxer Rising erupted with a siege of the Western embassies in Peking and the murder of the German ambassador. The embassies were never captured, and two months later the Great Powers sent in an international relief force to lift the siege. Once again China suffered the humiliation of an imposed treaty: the International Protocol of 1901, which required China to pay huge indemnities and to promise that any Chinese who joined an anti-foreign society would be summarily executed.

There had been surprisingly few casualties among the resident Europeans in Peking; but, in the countryside, it was a very different matter. There, it was the foreign missionaries – regarded as the agents of Western materialism and promoters of cultural aggression designed to destroy the traditional Chinese way of life – who bore the brunt of the Boxer fury. The Chinese converts to Christianity caught the lash with them.

More than 200 Western missionaries were slaughtered in that uprising, and something like 30,000 Chinese Christians are estimated to have perished at the hands of the Boxers. One of the Boxer edicts must have disturbed the sleep of thousands more: 'The Catholic and Protestant religions being insolent to the gods, and extinguishing sanctity, rendering no obedience to Buddha, and enraging Heaven and Earth, the rain clouds no longer visit us; but eight million Spirit soldiers will descend from Heaven and sweep the Empire clean of all foreigners . . .' It was a potent appeal to superstitious peasants worried about their harvests.

Less than a year after the Liddells were married, a certain Mrs Atwater of the American Board of Fenchow was writing home:

How am I to write all the horrible details of these days? The dear ones of Shouyang, seven in all, including our lovely girls, were taken prisoner and brought to Taiyuan in irons, and there by the Governor's orders beheaded, together with the Taiyuan friends, thirty-three souls.

The following days the Roman Catholic priests and nuns of Taiyuan were also beheaded, ten souls yesterday. Three weeks after these had perished, our mission at Taku was attacked, and our six friends there, and several brave Christians who stood by them, were beheaded. We are now waiting for our call home . . .

That was the China into which Eric Liddell was born, a China humiliated and torn by foreign intervention and moving inexorably towards revolution. It was in the same kind of China that Eric Liddell himself would die, forty-three years later, as a missionary in a Japanese internment camp when China, already in the throes of civil war, was occupied by invaders from Japan.

The Liddells had gone straight to the mission in Mongolia after their Shanghai wedding without even pausing for a honeymoon. Now, with the Boxer Rising convulsing northern China, they had to flee for their lives. Mrs Liddell was pregnant. They had to leave all their belongings except for one small trunk. Somehow they got to the coast safely after a number of alarming adventures, and took ship to Shanghai. There, in the London Missionary Society compound, Mary Liddell gave birth to their eldest son, Robert Victor. Three months later they again left for the north. Mrs Liddell was installed in the comparative safety of a missionary compound at the port of Tientsin, to the east of Peking, while her husband made his way back towards their former station in Mongolia to try to find out what had happened to the Christian community there.

Mrs Liddell wrote:

For four months he was touring Mongolia, with Colonel Wei and 200 soldiers, and I could get no word from him. I wish he had written down his experiences. He had a tale to tell that was thrilling, but never attempted to keep a diary. Life was too strenuous and it seemed we must just live a day at a time, as we never knew what would happen next . . . All winter was a difficult time, murders and horrible things happening.

It was there in Tientsin, on 16 January 1902, that their second son, Eric Henry Liddell, was born. The intention had been to christen him 'Henry Eric', but on the way to the church for the baptismal ceremony the order of names was hastily reversed when someone pointed out that the choice of initials – H.E.L. – would not be ideal for the son of a Christian missionary. That was Eric Liddell's story, anyway.

As a result of the Boxer Rising the mission in Mongolia had been abandoned, and Mr Liddell had been sent to a new posting at the village of Siaochang, in the province of southern Hopei, lying in the Great Plain of northern China, a vast expanse of fields and rivers dotted with little villages. It meant a difficult two-day journey, first by rail south to Techow (six hours), and then a forty-mile trek westwards on a bumpy Chinese cart drawn by two mules. As soon as the infant Eric was old enough to travel, Mrs Liddell took her two boys to join their father in Siaochang.

It is impossible not to be impressed by the casual courage of these missionaries and their wives and children. No journey was too daunting, no accommodation too uncomfortable. When the call came, they went.

Siaochang was one of the two mission stations in the Great Plain operated by the London Missionary Society. Between them they covered a population of about 10 million people, living in some 10,000 villages as close to one another, as one traveller put it, as currants in a fruit cake. Every square inch of soil was cultivated, with wheat and millet as the main crops. The climate veered wildly between the extremes of heat and cold, but at least it was mainly dry.

Missionary work had been going on in that vast area for many years, and the nucleus of a strong Chinese Church had begun to emerge with its own evangelists and teachers. The mission station in Siaochang itself then consisted of four large houses in a row, with verandas on two sides, both upstairs and down. Behind the houses were the church, a boys' school and a girls' school. The little complex was surrounded by a high mud wall, with a large gate that was closed at night.

Here, in 1903, the Liddells had their third child, a daughter called Jenny. Today she lives in Edinburgh, widow of a doctor, with two grown-up daughters; a slight figure, small and white-haired, soft-spoken and as gentle in manner as all the Liddells seem to have been. The youngest Liddell, a son called Ernest, was born some years later.

Jenny Liddell, now Mrs Jenny Somerville, has vivid memories of her early years in Siaochang. She remembers the devoted Chinese *amah* (nurse) who could not pronounce Eric's name properly and always called him 'Yellee'. The Liddells were the only European children in the compound, and they spent a lot of time playing with Chinese children dressed in their padded coats. The men, she remembers, still wore the traditional pigtail, imposed on the Chinese by the Manchu dynasty. She remembers her mother nursing the children through many illnesses, often with no doctor on hand. As a child, Eric once fell very ill indeed with fever, which left him for a long time extremely shaky on his legs; when he was up and about, one lady was overheard to make the immortal remark, 'That boy will never be able to run again!'

For two or three months each year when the summer heat was at its most intense, Mrs Liddell and the children would go to the seaside resort of Pei-tai-ho, on the Gulf of Pei-chili, where the mission had built a few cottages on the sea-front as holiday homes. Here they spent the summer months, swimming and lazing about, to be joined by Mr Liddell in August when 'his people' were all busy with their harvesting.

In 1907, Mr Liddell got his first furlough, after nine testing years in China, and returned to Scotland with his family. Eric was five years old at the time; it was the last time he would see Siaochang until he joined his elder brother Rob there in 1937 as a missionary himself.

Mr Liddell took a furnished house for his family in his home village of Drymen, where his father had been a greatly esteemed figure. D. P. Thomson, in his book *Scotland's Greatest Athlete*, cites a correspondent:

Eric's grandfather kept a small grocer's shop in Drymen. He also ran a small wagonette, locally known as 'Liddell's machine', to the railway station, about a mile from the village, to pick up any passengers (charge 6d.) or parcels. He was a bearded man, not given to much conversation. He always wore a high bowler hat (never a 'bunnet' like most countrymen), and his white pony ambled along the road at a pace which an active pedestrian could emulate.

The Liddells, a highly respected family, were noted for piety at a time and in a place where evangelism was considered unorthodox. I have a vague recollection of a group of evangelists who used to hold meetings in the village square. I think they belonged to the Faith Mission. The Liddells braved the criticism of their neighbours by coming out boldly in support of these visitors, singing Moody and Sankey hymns, etc.

This was the environment in which the Rev. James Dunlop Liddell had grown up, so it is perhaps not surprising that he should have chosen to devote his life to evangelism. And this was the family background with its traditions of personal conviction against which the two older Liddell boys, Rob and Eric, were to decide to become missionaries themselves.

Rob and Eric started their schooling in the village. But before Mr Liddell returned to China in the autumn of 1908, some more permanent arrangement had to be made, and the boys were sent to the School for the Sons of Missionaries in London which had been founded by the London Missionary Society in 1842. For Rob, aged eight, and Eric, not yet seven, it was the first taste of the family separation inherent in missionary life. The school, which was then at Blackheath, was to move to Mottingham in 1912 and change its name to Eltham College.

Eric made little impression at school to start with. One of his old masters recalled: 'When he first joined us, Eric was very shy, and, physically, rather "weedy". He missed his parents greatly, and sheltered as far as possible under his brother's protection . . . After two or three years his physique improved rapidly. W. B. Hayward, our headmaster, believed in plenty of fresh air, and two terms of hard "rugger" per year, with often three, or even four games per week, made of Eric a new man.'

It sounds very dated now, calling a ten-year-old schoolboy a 'man'; but this was at a time when 'Arnoldism', with its credo that sports were an integral part of character-formation, was in its heyday. The publication of *Tom Brown's Schooldays* by Thomas Hughes in the 1850s had presented a romanticized view of school games at the immortal Dr Thomas Arnold's Rugby School as an essential contribution to manliness, patriotism, moral character-building, stoicism, courage and team spirit. Dr H. H. Almond, the great nineteenth-century headmaster of Loretto School near Edinburgh, cried out in one of his celebrated sermons: 'Why, oh why, cannot there be a holy alliance between the athlete and the Christian; an alliance against the common enemies of both, against intemperance and indolence, and dissipation, and effeminacy, and aesthetic voluptuousness, and heartless cynicism, and all the unnatural and demoralizing elements in our social life?'

It was a passionate educational ideal certainly shared by W. B. Hayward, a strong disciplinarian, and his successor at Eltham College, George Robertson (later headmaster of George Watson's College in Edinburgh). At Eltham it was reinforced by the fact that nearly all the boys came from the same background: missionaries' sons, reared in a family atmosphere of quiet but determined piety. Eltham had its share of 'ragging' and bullying, of course, and Eric Liddell took his full schoolboy share in them; but he is also remembered by a fellow-schoolboy for putting a stop to the ragging of a new boy, a frightened and tearful 'man' of seven, when he was being forced to run the gauntlet of a double line of knotted handkerchiefs. Eric was all of eight years old at the time.

At school Eric was popular, though he always seemed a little detached and shy and never had a bosom pal. Academically he was competent, not brilliant. At sport, however, he shone; he once said to his sister, 'I don't think much of lessons, but I can run.' Not only could he run, but most sports came easily to him; his father had been an excellent gymnast in his day, and his elder brother Rob was also developing into a fine athlete. In fact, the rivalry on the sports field between the two brothers became one of the features of life at Eltham College. The results of the annual school sports in 1918, when Eric was sixteen and his brother nearly eighteen, make fascinating reading.

Cross Country Run:	1. R. V. Liddell	2. E. H. Liddell
Long Jump:	1. E. H. Liddell	2. R. V. Liddell
High Jump:	1. R. V. Liddell	2. E. H. Liddell
100 Yards	1. E. H. Liddell	2. R. V. Liddell
	(Equalled school record of 10·8 seconds)	
Hurdle Race:	1. R. V. Liddell	2. E. H. Liddell
Quarter Mile:	1. E. H. Liddell	2. R. V. Liddell

That year, Rob won the Senior Athletic Championship with 27 points to Eric's 23. Eric won it the following year, after Rob had left school, and in the course of it he set a new school record of 10·2 seconds for the 100 yards, which still stands unbroken.

It must be remembered that Eltham College was a relatively small school (only about 150 pupils), which made it fairly easy to shine, particularly during the First World War, when so many senior boys left early to go to the trenches. By 1916 Eric was playing cricket in the First XI ('Does not put enough force into his strokes,' commented the *Eltham College Magazine*). By 1918 he was vice-captain ('A good all-round cricketer'), and in 1919, at the age of eighteen, he was captain. Rugby was his real game, though, not cricket. He was in the First XV by the age of fourteen in 1916 ('A very light wing threequarter, but has not had much to do; he gets in some useful kicks which would prove better still if there were more strength behind them'). By 1917 he was 'a fast right wing threequarter, who has shown great improvement on last year. Tackling, kicking and falling on the ball are very good. Should do very well next year.' Next year he was captain of the XV at the age of only sixteen: 'He has captained the team with marked success throughout the season, and has been the mainstay of the three line. His kicking is excellent, and his speed and remarkable swerve have decided the issue of several matches. He is the best tackler, and the team is inclined to rely too much on him. He is inclined to be too lenient with the slacker of the team.'

The following year he was captain of both cricket and rugby, and a school prefect, too. And yet Eric Liddell was never *quite* as outstanding at school as we might have expected from his popularity and athletic prestige. For instance, he never became head boy, even though he did not leave school until he was nineteen. He never won the Bayard Prize, awarded annually by the vote of his school-fellows to the boy who had exerted the best influence during the year (Rob did, however). Surprisingly, both the Liddell brothers, talented as they were, had to give best to another outstanding pupil, A. Leslie Gracie, beside whom Eric would later play on the left wing in the Edinburgh University XV and during his brief career as a Scottish rugby international. Leslie Gracie always had the edge on them. Gracie became head boy. Gracie won the Bayard Prize. Gracie played rugby more dazzlingly than Eric, and cricket more effectively. In a trio of athletics champions, Gracie topped the lot by winning every single event on the sports programme on a single afternoon. Yet Eric Liddell the athlete is remembered everywhere, while Leslie Gracie as a sportsman is now a name familiar only to the real *aficionados* of Scottish rugby football.

Eric left Eltham College in the spring of 1920, needing one subject – French – to complete his entrance qualifications for

Edinburgh University, where brother Rob was already studying medicine. That summer, his mother came to Scotland on furlough with his sister Jenny and younger brother Ernest, and they all settled into a furnished house in Gillespie Crescent in Edinburgh. Eric 'crammed' hard and successfully, and in the autumn of 1920 he matriculated at the university for a B.Sc. degree in pure science, a four-year course with combined classes, both practical and theoretical, at Heriot-Watt College (now Heriot-Watt University) and the university itself. He was to prove himself an able student, especially at inorganic chemistry and mathematics, always near or at the top in his class-marks. Even in the Olympics year of 1924, when Eric was training hard on the race-track as well as studying for his Finals, his class-marks never fell below 68 per cent.

Eric Liddell's running career at the university started casually enough. He himself described it in the modest, throwaway style characteristic of the time: 'I had only been in the university a few months before the Athletic Sports came on. Six weeks before this event, a friend, hearing that I had done a little running at school, came round to try to persuade me to enter. I told him I was too busy. I had a lot of work to get through and no time for that sort of thing . . .'

In 1921 the Edinburgh University Athletic Club had just formed a separate Athletics Section, and interest in athletics was running high. Busy or not, Eric Liddell found the time to get in some training, and despite a six-day cycling tour to the top of Ben Nevis during the Easter vacation that left his legs stiff and aching, he entered for the University Sports that May. In the 100 and 220 yards the favourite was a former Stewart's College boy, G. Innes Stewart, who was being tipped as a future Scottish champion. Stewart himself described the two races in a special article in the *The Story of Edinburgh University Athletic Club*:

The last Saturday in May arrived, and we were soon trotting out for the 100-yards heats. Liddell was on my right, dressed in longish black pants and a white vest. Evan Hunter [the starter] got us off to a good start and I could see that I was not going to have it all my own way, for

Liddell was running me very close indeed and I reached the tape only a few inches in front of him. In the Final the reverse occurred, Liddell reaching the tape an inch or two in front of me. The time was 10·4 seconds.

My self-esteem was to get another rude shock in the furlong, generally considered my best distance. Liddell got off to a slightly better start and soon gained two yards on me. When we came to the last 80 yards I had narrowed the gap to about a yard, and finally got home by a matter of inches. The time, 23·4 seconds, was not remarkable, but on a slightly uphill grass track with little wind it was probably better than it looks.

After that I realized that a new power in Scottish athletics had arrived.

Eric Liddell, the unknown dark-horse freshman, had indeed arrived. His defeat in the 220 yards was to be the only time he ever lost a race in Scotland.

His performance that day won him a place in the Edinburgh University team for the Scottish Inter-University Sports, which meant putting in some serious training. He was taken to Powderhall, renowned for its dog racing. It was the first time he had run on a cinder track. Two or three times a week he would go there for training, practising starts and sprints on one side of the track to the accompaniment of the barking of excited whippets straining at the leash at the other side.

Training in those days was not the obsessive, all-consuming thing it is today for athletes with high aspirations. Eric Liddell trained regularly but not excessively, and there was hardly any coaching as we know it today. The first time he went to Powderhall he felt positively embarrassed at the sight of all the other runners dancing about on their toes as if they were stepping on hot bricks, working their shoulders, and bursting into ten-yard dashes. For university athletes, track-suits were unknown, and on a cold day they would remain in the pavilion until the last possible moment and then emerge, hoping that their overcoats would keep some of the wind from their bare legs below their knee-length shorts. Eric Liddell soon learned the vital importance of limbering up properly before a race – and slowing down gradually after one.

Liddell and Innes Stewart came first and second in the two sprints at the 1921 Inter-Universities Sports, to help give

Edinburgh a thumping win over Glasgow, Aberdeen and St Andrews. Soon Eric was winning races all over the place. In the 1922 Annual Sports at Edinburgh University, he won three sprint titles: the 100 yards in a wind-assisted time of 10·2 seconds that equalled the Sports best performance and the 220 yards (with no wind assistance) in 21·8 seconds, 0·2 second under the Scottish Native Record. Even more significantly, he won his first senior 440-yards race (the quarter-mile) in 52·6 seconds.

In the 1922 Scottish Championships he won the 100 and 220 yards, both in good times, and was awarded the Crabbie Cup for 'the most meritorious competitor in the season's Championship'. He was to win it again in 1923, 1924, and 1925 – an unparalleled achievement.

At the 1923 Inter-Universities Sports, he broke three records for the meeting. He won the 100 yards in 10·1 seconds (he had already equalled the Scottish record of 10·0 seconds), and the 220 yards in 21·6 seconds, which was a new Scottish Native Record. His time for the 440 yards, 50·2 seconds, remained an Inter-Universities record until 1957.

In the wake of all this record-breaking he was bringing home trophies right, left and centre from national and international meetings. His spoils of the chase were beginning to confound the ingenuity of his mother and sister in finding somewhere to put them all. 'Every week he would bring home prizes,' says his sister, Jenny Somerville. 'We were putting them under the bed in case they were stolen.' Among the winnings from that first 1921–2 season for which they had to find room in their new home in Merchiston Place were, not counting all the cups, a silver rose bowl, a cheese and biscuit dish, a three-tier cake stand, a large clock, a silver tea-set on a tray, a kettle, fish servers, silver brushes and combs, six tea-knives, fish-knives and forks, another six tea-knives, a flower vase, a leather suitcase, a travelling clock, a silver entrée dish, a case of cutlery, and a crop of watches. No one in the Liddell family would ever go short of a gold watch.

Contrary to the impression suggested by the film, *Chariots of Fire*, there was never any opposition from the family to his athletics. 'We were all thrilled to bits about his running,' says his sister Jenny, who feels a little hurt at being portrayed in the film as a rather schoolmarmish character who tried to get Eric to concentrate more on his religion. 'I was a naive, unsophisticated teenager at the time. I would never have dreamed of telling Eric what to do.'

Eric was meanwhile notching up rugby successes to add to his athletic triumphs. In his second year at university he was playing for the First XV at centre threequarter, impressing everyone with his blazing speed and determination. Within a couple of months, in his first season of playing senior rugby, he was featuring in the international Trials, playing on the left wing outside his former schoolboy partner, Leslie Gracie, who had matured into a centre threequarter of devastating pace and elusiveness. In the two Trials, Liddell scored no fewer than ten tries. *The Scotsman* commented magisterially on the first game: 'This game will long be remembered by those present for the brilliant combination which A. L. Gracie and E. H. Liddell made ... The pair give promise of being the fastest wing Scotland ever had.' After the second Trial, *The Scotsman* was even more effusive about Eric Liddell:

His great speed is not his only asset; for not only did he 'round' one, and sometimes two, opponents when he scored, but time and again he had to use both resource and initiative. Never once was he found wanting. He showed an almost uncanny intuition for being in the right place at the right time, and no matter how unconventional Gracie might be in some of his offensive tactics, Liddell refused to be taken by surprise, as quite excusably he might have been. He has learned the use of the reverse pass, and in defence he is improving with every game he plays.

After the Trials, the selection of the 'Gracie–Liddell wing' was a virtual certainty. In the next two seasons, they were to play seven times together for Scotland, during which Scotland lost only once (the 1923 Calcutta Cup match against England at Inverleith Place, Edinburgh), before Eric retired from rugby to concentrate on athletics. It was a record that any internationalist would be proud of: seven games, only one lost. Yet there is something perplexing, oddly inconsistent, about his career as an international rugby player – something missing somewhere, as with his career at school. Despite his tremendous speed, despite his courage in the tackle, and his celebrated swerve, his game seldom really 'came off'. *The Scotsman* vacillated between praise and faint praise. Against Ireland in 1922: 'That he is a great player in the making there is no doubt, but there were times when he showed a rawness in his work and lack of resource when cornered.' Against France in 1923: 'The Gracie–Liddell wing was as meteoric and mercurial as ever; Liddell was the more efficient of the two, and seemed to be putting more fire in his play than is his wont.' Against Wales at the Arms Park, Cardiff, in 1923: 'Gracie was the vital, living force in the threequarter line. His partner on the wing, E. H. Liddell, improves every game he plays. He runs now with more determination than he showed last year, and he showed real grit and some football on several occasions. Had he a less extraordinary man beside him, he might be much more dangerous than he is ever allowed to be.'

This was the occasion of one of Scotland's most famous victories over Wales in Cardiff, by 11–8. It was Scotland's first win there since 1890, and after the game was over, the Scottish threequarters were actually carried shoulder-high off the field by their sporting Welsh opponents.

In his last international, the Calcutta Cup game with England, there was more than just the disappointment of defeat: 'The Scottish threequarter line was not seen to advantage. Nothing can be urged against Liddell. He got few chances, and, although hardly so prominent as against Ireland, he ran with fine resolution.'

Like many a 'speed-merchant' in rugby, Liddell has sometimes been thought of as simply a sprinter, not a footballer. Yet, paradoxically, he loved rugby more than any of the other sports which he enjoyed. The sporting journalist William A. Reid summed it up shrewdly: 'Liddell liked running, but he loved football. For all that, he was not a natural footballer, as he was a natural runner, and although he was too plucky and too good a tackler to be stigmatized as a "mere sprinter", he had not the attributes, the knack, and the craft of the great football player.'

With the merest hint of sisterly bias, Jenny Somerville puts it this way: 'Eric, unfortunately, got a reputation, so there was always somebody to spot him and mark him; so he never got the chance he might have had if he had not been marked so closely. Anyway, he gave up rugger because he started concentrating on his running.'

Yet amongst all the rugby, the running and the studying, something else, something even more important, was happening in Eric Liddell's life. It came to a head on the day his friend and future biographer, the Rev. Dr D. P. Thomson, invited him to speak at a Christian evangelistic meeting in Armadale, an industrial town in West Lothian in the central belt of Scotland. The meeting was to be part of a vigorous campaign in central Scotland that was being run by the Glasgow Students' Evangelistic Union, which had been founded the year before. Thomson was deputed to ask Eric Liddell, already the best-known athlete in Scotland, to come and address a special meeting for men only in the Town Hall. His brother Rob was already involved in this interdenominational student crusade, and it was believed that Eric himself was even now contemplating the possibility of work overseas. D. P. travelled to Edinburgh (hitch-hiking on a lorry) and went straight to the Edinburgh Medical Mission Hostel at 56 George Square, where Eric and Rob were now lodging after their family had returned to China. Thomson put the proposition to him, directly. Eric dropped his head for a moment to consider it, and then said, 'All right – I'll come.'

That meeting at Armadale was a watershed in Eric Liddell's life, because it was the first public confession of the Christian faith which was to inform the rest of his life so vividly. Until then it had been a private matter. At school he had been a regular member of the weekly Bible class, where attendance was wholly voluntary, but he had never taken part in any of the discussions. In due time he had become a full communicant member of the Church at the age of fifteen, helped to form a branch of the Crusaders' Union at the school, and assisted in the work of the Islington Medical Mission. His faith had always been firm but unspoken. It seems to have been real to him virtually from childhood, taught by his parents and accepted by their children. Eric had found his own answer to the universe at an age long before most people realize there is a question – and he never saw any reason to doubt it.

No one ever talks of Eric Liddell expressing 'doubts'. He never seemed to be greatly exercised by any of the nagging intellectual questions that have so often ruffled the serenity of the modern believer. His wife, Florence, says that he may have had doubts, but he never spoke of them. He read voraciously, she says, and often felt discouraged. But doubts? On the whole, she thinks not: 'It was a simple, personal faith.' Was this naivety? Perhaps it was. Or perhaps it was an intellectual innocence that apprehends truths with a child-like clarity that eludes the worldly-wise. It is difficult to tell with a man like Eric Liddell. He was so much the product of a particular missionary family and a particular religious tradition; yet he would invest that inheritance with a distinctive character that transcended the stereotype.

His faith was rooted deep in the evangelical fundamentalist tradition, which accepts the Bible not just as a collection of wise maxims and cautionary tales but as the embodiment of the truth about mankind, about man's destiny and his relationship with God.

The principle of keeping the seventh day of the week holy as a day of rest, which was soon to hurl Eric Liddell into international prominence, springs from these beliefs. Principles like that had been instilled into him from boyhood, and his nature was not that of the restless questioner. He listened, he accepted, and then, like the perfectionist he always was, he worked on it until his faith was so deeply a part of the cast of his mind and personality that he came to live his life in a way which people, reminiscing over his incandescent memory, would over and over again call Christ-like.

His was not an intellectual faith of the metaphysical wrestling-match kind. But its transmutation of his life has a way of withering intellectual questions and making you wonder if these questions ever really mattered. He achieved a special serenity of a different kind. Pain, for instance, pain suffered by others, troubled him deeply; but when he encountered it in its most hideous forms in war-ravaged China in the 1930s and 1940s, he didn't use it as an intellectual weapon against God and sit back to brood over the latest cosmic grimace. He simply transformed pain into a vindication of love.

Eric Liddell leaves you wondering, at the end, whether he perhaps had his finger on a stronger pulse than have all the intellectuals, empiricists and trendy theologians put together.

That first public evangelical meeting at Armadale on 6 April 1923 was the beginning of a life of dedicated service to God. There were only some seventy or eighty men present, but they listened attentively. Eric Liddell had that sort of effect on people. In the evangelical campaigns that followed his début at Armadale, culminating in his year of public speaking after the 1924 Olympics, people came flocking to listen to him. Of course, the press had something to do with that, for Eric Liddell was the Scottish superstar of the 1920s, a celebrity who could always attract an audience. Yet it was not his fame alone that explains his attraction – especially in view of the fact that he was rather a poor speaker in public. He was quiet, he was diffident, he was really rather monotonous. His huge audiences were certainly not mesmerized by oratory. He did not have a special way with words. And this makes it all the more remarkable that, wherever he went, whether in Scotland or later in China, he could command such rapt attention. It was the genuine power of his personality that drew people, the compulsion of his belief, the down-to-earth quality of his sincerity. People were made aware of a strength they couldn't quite put a finger on. Eric Liddell talked about ordinary things, without rhetoric – what he had done that day, what he felt about this and that. He told them that Jesus could make a difference to the way they lived their lives tomorrow. He told them that the Kingdom of Heaven was God living inside them, and that this was where the power to have faith came from, and the power to run a race well – simple things like that.

He had the common touch, the ability to talk to anyone like a friend and make that person feel both important – and challenged. That must be why no one who recalls even the most fleeting contact with Eric Liddell has anything less than the most fulsome tribute to pay to him. Whether it was a Chinese coolie, an Olympic Games masseur, a Glasgow down-and-out, a Japanese soldier, a schoolgirl with a crush, a teenager who wanted her hockey-stick mended again, a hospital matron, a nagging colleague – Eric had the same smile for them all. It all sounds too good to be true. But then, the truth sometimes is.

His behaviour at athletic meetings is a case in point. Those who remember him from those days rarely talk of his running without adding something about the kind of man he was. His first major opponent at the University Sports in 1921, Innes Stewart, wrote, 'He was very modest, rather shy, and most pleasant to talk to.'

Neil Campbell, now Emeritus Professor of Chemistry at Edinburgh University, was a fellow-member of the Athletic Club and used to race against Eric. On one occasion, he remembers, Eric offered to exchange the places they had drawn for the 440 yards. Neil Campbell was drawn in the outside lane, and in those days there was no 'stagger' to the lanes at domestic meetings – everyone had to make a mad scramble for the inside of the track after the gun. Eric Liddell, knowing that he was the more experienced of the two, was quite happy to give his fellow-competitor the advantage of the inside track. Professor Campbell writes: 'No athlete has ever made a bigger impact on people all over the world, and the description of him as "the most famous, the most popular, and best-loved athlete Scotland has ever produced" is no exaggeration.'

The stories of Eric Liddell from this time are full of tales of his chivalry on the race-track. It is difficult to tell them without making him sound insufferably well-meaning, though this does not seem to have been how the gestures came across to his fellow-competitors. There is the story of how he went up to speak to a black runner whom no one else was speaking to, and engaged him in conversation. There was the way he would offer his opponents the trowel he used to dig holes for starting, and then shake hands with them all before the race. No one seems to have wished that 'Liddell and that damn trowel of his' would go away. His chivalry seems to have been accepted as naturally as it was offered.

By this time the 1924 Olympic Games were getting nearer, and speculation was mounting as to which sprinters would represent Great Britain. As late as June 1923, Eric Liddell had not been seen on a running-track in London, and the short-distance times he had been recording in Scotland were still inconsistent enough to make his Olympic selection a matter of some doubt. But his performance at the AAA Championships at Stamford Bridge in London that July changed all that. Eric ran like a man inspired. He won the 220 in 21·6 seconds, and won the 100 in a new British record of 9·7 seconds. That record would not be broken for thirty-five years (Peter Radford in 1958 in 9·6 seconds) – which makes it one of the longest-standing records in British athletics.

If that was not enough to clinch his selection for the British Olympics team, then his performance at Stoke-on-Trent the following week certainly was. That was the week-end that Eric, representing Scotland in the Triangular Contest with England and Ireland, won all three sprints – the 100, the 220 and the 440 yards. That triple win was in itself a unique achievement; but it was his astonishing performance in the 440 yards which has gone down in the annals of athletics.

There he was, three strides into the race, when suddenly he was stumbling on to the grass. J. J. Gillies of England, bursting through for the inside berth, had knocked Eric off the track. For a moment he hesitated, thinking he was disqualified. But a number of officials signalled him urgently to continue and spectators watched, mesmerized, as he sprang forward again and went pounding after his opponents. By now they were twenty yards ahead of him. Surely he could never make up that kind of distance?

Arms swinging, fists punching the air, head thrown back, he began to draw up on the leaders. He was fourth now, ten yards behind Gillies. Forty yards from home he was still only third and on the point of collapse. But with another superhuman effort, incredibly, he was there. He was first. He had beaten Gillies by two yards and his time was 51·2 seconds. He had given a top-class field a start of twenty yards – two seconds – and won. He collapsed in exhaustion at the tape. It was one of the great races of all time, and the crowd rose to him as he was carried from the field. As *The Scotsman* said next day: 'The circumstances in which he won it made it a performance bordering on the miraculous. Veterans whose memories take them back thirty-five years, and in some cases even longer, in the history of athletics, were unanimous in the opinion that Liddell's win in the quarter-mile was the greatest track performance they had ever seen.'

He ran that day, everyone said, like a man inspired. But, in fact, he should never have won a race at all. Modern coaches would have been appalled at his running style. It was like his public speaking – poor. His old opponent, Innes Stewart, put it politely: 'Liddell had a curious action, swinging his arms very high, bringing his knees well up, and throwing his head well back.'

In fact his arms were waving around like windmills. He attacked the air, he clawed the air, he punched the air. His chin was up, his head was so far back he seemed to be gazing at the sky. He wobbled a bit as he ran, too. But that extraordinary style propelled him towards the finishing tape faster than anyone else in the world. And the exhilaration on his face as he ran! The exultation on his face as he threw back his head! People never forgot their first sight of Eric Liddell running at full stretch.

A fascinating insight into his style comes from Ian Charleson, the actor who plays Eric Liddell in the film, *Chariots of Fire*. 'Liddell's style was a problem,' he said. 'I had to learn to run properly and then to learn Liddell's way. The hardest thing was that Eric ran with his head back, but when I did it I couldn't see where I was going. I kept running off the track and bumping into other runners.

'Then one day, on the fifth or sixth day of filming, I suddenly cottoned on to what he must have been doing when he ran. At drama school we used to do what are called "trust exercises", where you run as hard as you can towards a wall and trust someone will stop you, or you fall off a piano and trust someone will catch you.

'I suddenly realized – Liddell must have run like that. He must have run with his head up and literally trusted to get there. He ran with faith. He didn't even look where he was going. So I can see how that would have given him a lot of extra push in a way. He just let go, completely relaxed.'

That moment when he threw his head back and opened his mouth and set his chin, was the moment Eric found something extra. At an athletics championship at Hampden Park in

Glasgow, a spectator once remarked to the bowler-hatted Glaswegian next to him that Liddell would be hard put to it to win this race. It was the last lap of the 440 yards and Liddell – often a poor starter – had forty yards to make up.

'*His heid's no' back yet*', was the laconic reply. Whereupon, as the spectator reported later, back went the head and Liddell left his opponents standing to win by twenty yards.

Where he got that extra push from when his head went back is anyone's guess. His sister tells the story that when someone asked him the secret of his success at 440 yards, he said: 'The first half I run as fast as I can, and the second half I run faster with God's help.'

Just as typical of the man is the reply quoted by Bob Knight, a former ship's engineer from Tyneside who used to call in on Eric years later when his ship docked in China. Bob was with Eric once when someone was introduced to the famous athlete and commented on how frequently he had looked as if he was going to lose a race and suddenly came away with a burst of speed. The guest, and the assembled company, waited for Eric to tell them how he put up a prayer or called on the Lord. Something suitably pious, anyway. But, according to Bob Knight, 'He smiled that quiet smile of his – I can picture him now – and he said, "The fact is, I don't like to be beaten".'

That is also what Eric told his running mates the day they were out jogging and a corporation bus drew alongside and hooted a challenge. No one but Eric had the energy for that last, uphill spurt. He raced after the bus and beat it to the top of the hill. 'I don't like to be beaten,' he explained when the others caught him up.

Eric Liddell didn't like to be beaten. That explains the set of his teeth, the way he fought the air, the determination to stretch his body to the limits, the grit that took him off the ground when he fell and hurled himself to the finishing line. But it doesn't invalidate Ian Charleson's discovery that he ran, in a sense, by faith. Faith requires some input from the believer.

D. P. Thomson has insisted that, in the three months after the public confession of his faith at Armadale, Liddell ran more brilliantly and achieved greater distinction as a sprinter than ever before. It may be true. Liddell didn't like to be beaten, but his was no compulsive lust for victory. He wasn't trying to prove anything, to be a star, to show the world. He loved running, he exulted in it, his body, mind and soul were in it together. So if his spirit was liberated, it's no wonder he threw his head back and found new resources of strength in his legs and his lungs as well.

Whether he could have been the same runner today under the constraints of modern sport is something else. His diet would certainly have appalled a modern trainer. Eric was living with twelve or thirteen others in the Edinburgh Medical Mission, so he just ate what they were given. He tried to avoid too much heavy food on the day of a race, but that wasn't always possible.

'On one day on which I ran, I took plum pudding,' he said later, 'and that day I ran the second fastest "quarter" I have ever run in Scotland.'

Whatever he ate before a race, Eric was now a certainty for the 1924 Olympics in Paris. He would run in the 100-metre sprint, at which he had always excelled and was reigning British Champion, and the 200 metres. The 100 metres was the jewel of the Games and Eric wanted to win it.

Then the timetables came out. The 100 metre heats were on a Sunday.

2

'I'm Not Running on a Sunday'

'I'm not running,' he said, and nothing would budge him. He didn't make a fuss, but he was absolutely firm about it. The Sabbath was God's day, and he would not run. Not even in the Olympic Games.

The British athletics authorities were horrified. It was early in 1924, only a few months before the Eighth Olympics in Paris, and Eric Liddell was Britain's main hope for the 100 metres. He was their golden boy. And now he was saying he would not run in the qualifying heats of the 100 metres because they were being held on a Sunday. It was tantamount to throwing away a gold medal for Scotland, and for Britain.

Eric made his decision known as soon as the timetables for the Olympics were announced. 'It was all very quiet,' says his fellow student athlete, Professor Neil Campbell. 'Liddell was the last person to make a song and dance about that sort of thing. He just said, "I'm not running on a Sunday" – and that was that. And he would have been very upset if anything much had been made of it at the time. We thought it was completely in character, and a lot of the athletes were quietly impressed by it. They felt that here was a man who was prepared to stand for what he thought was right, without interfering with anyone else, and without being dogmatic or anything like that. Quietly, he just said, "I'm not running on a Sunday." '

Jenny Somerville, Eric's sister, doesn't think it was a tortuously difficult decision for him to make at the time. The Olympics were still some months ahead – not, as popular legend has it, on the morrow. It was not a dramatic, last-minute change of mind, as some sports writers have suggested. Eric Liddell, and the sporting authorities, had known for a long time that he could not, and would not, compete in the 100 metres if the heats were to be run on a Sunday.

Reverence for the Sabbath was as natural to Eric Liddell as breathing, and infinitely more precious than a gold medal. It probably didn't occur to him to try to rationalize it. Or did he have doubts? Did he try to persuade himself that he would be honouring God just as much by winning a race for Him as by having a Sabbath rest? Did he perhaps wonder if it would not be a finer thing to sacrifice his principles just this once for the sake of a gold for Scotland? But if these thoughts ever occurred to Eric Liddell, he did not voice them, or let them stay very long. Nor did he let press criticism or public jibes about 'national honour' change his mind, even though he was hurt by the comments and deeply unhappy about denying Scotland a rare and precious chance of excelling in the Blue Riband event of the Olympics.

'He was called a traitor to his country, and I think he felt it quite keenly,' says his wife Florence, to whom he told the story many years later. But he had the support of many athletes, one of whom was so impressed by Eric's stand that he actually followed his example at another race meeting some time after the Olympics. The man was Tom Riddell, eight times the Scottish champion miler between 1925 and 1935. He used to run in medley relay races with Eric, with Riddell on the half-mile leg and Liddell on the quarter-mile. He describes Eric as 'a terrific influence on all of us athletes at the time' – so much so that when Tom Riddell was chosen to run in a race-meeting in Italy, and learned that the race was to be run on a Sunday morning, he withdrew. 'That was because of Eric's example,' he says. 'Without the slightest doubt, Eric Liddell was the greatest athlete Scotland has ever produced – by his influence, his example and his capabilities.'

Eric had also declined to run in the Olympic 4×100 and the

4×400 metre relays, for which he had been selected; their heats, too, were to be run on a Sunday. But it was his refusal to run in the 100 metres that was the real blow to the athletic authorities. Only the previous year he had established himself as one of the fastest men in the world, when he won the AAA sprint double in 9·7 seconds for the 100 yards and 21·6 seconds for the 220. His time for the 100 yards had been only a tenth of a second short of the world record, and no British sprinter would excel it for another thirty-five years. It was little wonder that he had been hailed as the man who could capture the Olympic 100 metres crown for Britain for the first time since the Games had been revived in 1896.

With Eric Liddell's withdrawal, British hopes now switched to Harold Abrahams, a Jewish student who had been notching up steadily improving times for Cambridge University and in national contests. But no one, least of all Abrahams himself, was unduly optimistic about his Olympic chances. There would be a formidable team of American sprinters in Paris, with a flush of superior times among them. Abrahams had a 9·9 second 100 yard time to his credit – equivalent to between 10·7 and 10·8 seconds for the 100 metres. But Charles Paddock of the United States, the reigning Olympic champion, had been unofficially credited with 10·2 for the slightly longer 110 yards. So Abrahams had little cause to feel particularly confident.

Harold Abrahams was the son of a Lithuanian Jew, and born in 1899. His was an exceptionally athletic family: his elder brother Sidney won the AAA long-jump title in 1913. Harold's own running début was at Stamford Bridge, London, then the mecca of British athletics, at the age of ten. In 1918 he began to make a name for himself by winning both the 100 yards and the long jump at the Public Schools Championships (he went to Repton). During a short spell of army service, he raced against his boyhood hero, the legendary sprinter Willie Applegarth, who had won a bronze in the 200 metres at the Stockholm Olympics of 1912; Lieutenant Abrahams was given a start of two yards on the twenty-nine-year-old champion – and beat him by six yards in 10·0 seconds. Later that year (1919), Abrahams went up to Cambridge to study law at Caius College, and launched himself on a dazzling student athletics career. Between 1920 and 1923 he won an unprecedented eight out of nine events in the annual athletics contests with Oxford; in his final appearance in the 'Battle of the Blues', he won the 100 yards in 10·0 seconds, the 440 yards in a career best of 50·8 seconds, and the long jump with an English Native Record of 23 feet 7¼ inches.

Much of the passionate zeal he put into his running was fired, he was later to claim, by the alleged anti-semitism he encountered at Cambridge. Caius College has been greatly piqued by the elaboration of this theme in the *Chariots of Fire* film, and declined to co-operate with the shooting of the Cambridge scenes. The college strongly refutes the allegations of anti-semitism in the 1920s. This uneasy relationship between Abrahams (who died in 1978) and his Alma Mater makes an interesting contrast with that of Eric Liddell and Edinburgh University, who not only fêted their favourite graduand in 1924 but honoured his memory fulsomely with a Gala performance of *Chariots of Fire* in the spring of 1981.

During the winter of 1923–4, Abrahams trained hard with an eye to the Olympics. Four years previously he had been selected for the Antwerp Olympics while still a freshman at Cambridge, only to be eliminated in the second round of the 100 metres heats. This time he was determined to do a lot better; and who better to help him do that than Sam Mussabini, the coach who had already trained those fine Polytechnic Harriers sprinters, Willie Applegarth and Harry Edward (winner of the Olympic bronze medal for the 200 metres at Antwerp in 1920). When Harold Abrahams trained under Sam Mussabini's severe eye, he really trained: three times a week he was hard at it – and that was above average for those days – paying a meticulous attention to the mechanics of running that was far ahead of its time.

He recalled later:

Sam was 'dead nuts' – that was the expression he used – on the arm action, with the arms kept low, bent at the elbows (we used running corks for a good grip): he maintained, which I believe to be absolutely sound, that the action of the arms very largely controls the poise of the body and action of the legs. My training sessions consisted largely of perfecting the start and practising arm action over and over again. There were no starting blocks in those days, and we took meticulous care with the placing and digging of holes and the accurate control of the first few strides. I always carried a piece of string the length of the first stride, and marked the spot on the track, at which I gazed intently on the word 'set'.

Our partnership was ideal, because Sam was not an autocrat. We discussed theory for many hours and argued and argued until I accepted that his theories were sound – not because of his experience and knowledge, but because my mind was satisfied with his reasons. We paid infinite attention to my length of stride multiplied by the rapidity with which a stride is taken. I used to put down pieces of paper on the track at measured distances and endeavour to pick them up with my spikes as I ran. I shall always believe that the vital factor in my running in Paris was that by conscientious training I had managed to shorten my stride an inch or two and get an extra stride into my 100 metres. Then Sam encouraged me to work on a 'drop' finish. [A 'drop' finish meant that dipping lunge at the end of a race to get your chest to the tape first in a tight finish.]

The contrast with Liddell is irresistible. There was Eric, down at Powderhall among all those yapping whippets a couple of nights a week, or maybe three times if he weren't preaching fifty miles away. His arm action alone would have driven Mussabini 'dead nuts'. Add the hands, the legs, the sky-gazing head and the wobble – and the celebrated coach would have given up in despair. It is hard, too, to imagine Liddell concluding that the vital factor in his Olympic chances would have anything to do with the shortening of a stride by dint of conscientious training. Liddell certainly worked at his running, but the secret of his Paris win, when it came, was inside him. Whatever it was that could lift Liddell to his astonishing feats of athletic achievement – whether it was the spirit within him, the pain and the joy and the longing and the love, or something else – it had nothing to do with counting strides.

Liddell and Abrahams never raced against each other, although they had been expected to meet in the AAA championships at Stamford Bridge in 1923. But Abrahams, suffering from a septic throat that day, failed to reach the final. Liddell did reach it. That was the day he won the 100 yards in 9·7 seconds and became Britain's great hope for the Olympics.

Liddell, however, was now out of the Olympic 100 metres

sprint. The problem was what on earth to do with him. In the end he was asked to train instead for the 400 metres in Paris. And that was how Eric Liddell discovered that he was a natural quarter-miler.

Of course, his amazing recovery and victory in the Triangular Contest race at Stoke-on-Trent in 1923 had shown he could run the 440 yards if he felt like it. But he had never trained seriously for it; it had never been considered 'his race'. Conventional sporting wisdom had it that the 100 and the 200 metres went together in an athlete's training, as did the 400 and the 800. So perhaps the man who would be hailed as 'the world's finest quarter-miler' might never have fulfilled his potential if an insuperable obstacle in the shape of Eric Liddell's conscience had not overturned all the traditionally accepted ideas about it, and turned the 400 from a middle-distance race into a sprint.

'Eric always said that the great thing for him,' his wife Florence recalls, 'was that when he stood by his principles and refused to run in the 100 metres, he found that the 400 metres was really his race. He said he would never have known that otherwise. He would never have dreamed of trying the 400 at the Olympics.'

The quarter-mile, or the 400 metres (there is a difference of only about two metres between them), is one of the most demanding races that exists. A more recent British Olympic star, Adrian Metcalfe, has described it as 'a sprint which also possesses those features one admires most in middle-distance events: stamina, the need to fight till the tape, the virtual masochism of pleasure through prolonged pain – a race in which one's body reaches to one's internal conflict. Physically the race is simple. But to make oneself do it . . . that is the challenge which, if overcome, yields the tremendous satisfaction.'

It has always been a glamour event, in which the unexpected has become almost expected. More than fifty years earlier, in 1868, a brilliant runner called Edward Colbeck had won the quarter-mile at the English Championships under the most bizarre circumstances. Half-way through the race, which was being run on the Beaufort House field in West London, a sheep wandered on to the track. Colbeck crashed into it, breaking the poor creature's leg and losing about eight yards (about a second in time). Yet he clocked up 50·4 seconds, his best-ever run. It would be nearly twenty years before the runner broke the magic 50 second mark with 49·8 in winning the AAA title in 1886 – an achievement as notable in its time as Roger Bannister's breaking of the four-minute barrier in the mile at Oxford in 1954.

The 400 metres had not been a particular British speciality in the early Olympics. In the very first Olympics, at Athens in 1896, Britain's second string, Gilbert Jordan, had won the silver, close behind the American winner, Thomas Burke. In the Fourth Olympics, the London-born Scot, Lieutenant Wyndham Halswelle of the Highland Light Infantry, won the gold medal at the newly opened White City stadium in the saddest of circumstances. In the final, which he was contesting as favourite against three Americans, J. C. Carpenter of the USA was disqualified for bumping and boring in the home straight. A re-run was ordered, the other Americans boycotted the race in protest, and Halswelle was left to run the distance solo to win the gold medal in a time of 50·0 seconds – well below his previous best of 48·4.

By Eric Liddell's day, the 400 metres (or 440 yards, as it was usually run in Britain) was becoming a British preserve – or at least an Olympic event for which British hopes could reasonably stand high. In the Olympic year of 1920, two student runners at Oxford and Cambridge, Guy Butler and the South African Rhodes scholar Bevil Rudd, were vying for world supremacy after dead-heating in the annual Oxford *v*. Cambridge match in 49·6 seconds. In the Olympics themselves, on a rain-sodden track at Antwerp, Rudd snatched the gold, again in 49·6 against Butler, who was closing on him fast. That silver medal was the first of four Olympic medals that Butler would win in his outstanding career.

In 1924, British hopes once again rested with Guy Butler; Liddell wasn't rated as anything more than an outsider. Unfortunately Butler suffered continuously from a 'game' leg which seriously handicapped his distinguished career as a runner; when the Olympics came round, his thigh was heavily bandaged and he had to start from an upright position instead of using the faster crouching start.

Eric Liddell trained hard in the few months left to him before the big race. His blood was up now, but he had a long way to go.

At the AAA Championships, held within a few weeks of the Olympics, he had fended off British, Canadian and American opposition to win in the respectable time of 49·6 seconds. But his chances of beating the cluster of Olympic entrants, all of whom were credited with times around 48 seconds, looked extremely remote.

The Paris Games ushered in a new era in the Olympic movement. They opened on Saturday, 5 July 1924 to a crowd of about 60,000. There were forty-four nations competing this time, fifteen more than at Antwerp, and more than 3,000 participants, some 500 more than last time. The Americans alone had a contingent of 400, who did things in style by arriving in a liner and a battleship with a flamboyant retinue of trainers, coaches, masseurs, managers and a chaplain. In track and field events, six world records would be set that year and fifteen Olympic records equalled or surpassed. The swimmers would set two world records and equal or beat ten previous Olympic marks; one of their stars was the great Johnny Weissmuller, who won three gold medals (and another two in 1928) and went on to make his name and fortune as the screen Tarzan.

The Olympic motto, *Citius, altius, fortius* ('Faster, higher, stronger') was coined for these Games by a sports-loving French schoolmaster. Huts appeared for the first time around the stadium – not exactly an Olympic village, but at least a step in the direction of collective accommodation. Women competed in fencing for the first time; and lawn tennis and rugby football saw their last Olympics.

But the thing that everyone would remember the 1924 Olympics for was the searing heat. Never before had the Games been staged in the sort of heat in which the Colombes Stadium sweltered that month of July. A 'cauldron', some called the stadium – others preferred 'furnace'; and one of the refreshment stalls was dubbed *La Bonne Frite* ('The Good Fry'). On some days the temperature was as high as 45°C (113°F). Runners in the 10,000 metres cross-country race were dropping like flies, and only twenty-three of the thirty-eight starters finished the course.

The 2nd Queen's Own Cameron Highlanders were stationed in Cologne at the time, and were sent to Paris as the official

British musicians for the Olympics. Their first duty was to lead the march of the British athletes up the Champs-Elysées to lay a wreath at the tomb of the Unknown Warrior. HRH Edward, Prince of Wales, laid the wreath, and four pipers played that infinitely poignant lament 'The Flowers of the Forest', which mourns the calamitous Scottish defeat at the Battle of Flodden in 1513.

Captain Philip Christison was in charge that day. In the front row of the party of British athletes he noticed his fellow Scot, Eric Liddell – someone he would see a good deal more of that week, because they had both found themselves staying at the same Hôtel du Louvre. Captain Christison had the task of getting Liddell and the other British athletes to the stadium in time for their events. Despite the innovation of huts near the stadium, many of the athletes were still scattered in hotels all over the city. The Americans complicated the process by carrying their competitive spirit to the streets, and monopolizing the taxis at higher fares than anyone else would offer. The harassed British captain had to resort to stopping private cars in the street and pleading with the drivers to get the athletes to the race in time. The Olympics were a lot of fun in those days.

Liddell and the captain met from time to time in the hotel lounge for a chat, and Eric confided to him that his decision not to run in the 100 metres still weighed heavily on his mind.

'I wonder if I'm doing the right thing?' he would say. But he always added a minute later, 'No, I'm sure I'm right.' The captain, now General Sir Philip Christison, says Eric was still under pressure from his team-mates to run the 100 metres. There was no acrimony in it, but Eric felt keenly that he was letting his country down. It was so rare for a Scot to reach this class in athletics and, yes, he felt it.

He was hardly allowed to forget that his behaviour was considered to have been 'less than cricket'. Lord Cadogan, who was among the numerous British dignitaries at the Games, had given the team a little pep-talk at the start: 'To play the game is the only thing in life that matters,' he had said. Was he aware of Eric Liddell's eyes on him as he said it? Whether or not his words were an implicit rebuke to Liddell, *The Scotsman* heaped its own coals of fire when it reported them the next day. 'There is not the least doubt,' said the paper, 'that the British team will play up and play the game, thus upholding the honour and reputation of Great Britain.'

On the day when he should have been on the sprint track doing what Lord Cadogan considered the only thing in life that matters, Eric Liddell was preaching at a Scots church in another part of Paris. The film *Chariots of Fire* shows him preaching on a text from the prophet Isaiah. And Isaiah's commentary on man's vain bid to 'go it alone' is made to resound round the little church while the athletes are seen pounding the track on the other side of the city.

'Hast thou not known, hast thou not heard,' cries the screen Eric Liddell, 'that the everlasting God, the Lord, the Creator of the ends of the earth, fainteth not, neither is weary? . . . He giveth power to the faint: and to them that have no might he increaseth strength. Even the youths shall faint and be weary, and the young men shall utterly fall.' His voice rises. 'But they that wait upon the Lord shall renew their strength; they shall mount up with wings as eagles; they shall run, and not be weary; and they shall walk, and not faint.'

There is not a scrap of evidence that the real-life Eric Liddell actually preached anything of the kind. Besides, he would hardly have carried it off with anything like the flair of Ian Charleson, for he was a mediocre orator. But he must have known the passage well, and he would no doubt have loved to quote it back at Lord Cadogan.

On the following day, Monday, 7 July, Liddell was back in the Stade Colombes to cheer Harold Abrahams on to victory in the semi-final and final of the 100 metres. Abrahams settled his feet in the starting-holes (starting-blocks were not patented until 1927), with the words echoing in his mind that Sam Mussabini had written to him in a note just before the Games opened: 'Only think of two things – the report of the pistol and the tape. When you hear the one, just run like hell till you break the other.' Abrahams did just that, and burst through the tape with his celebrated 'drop-finish' at 10·6 seconds, with Jackson Scholz of the USA less than a metre behind, and Arthur Porritt of New Zealand winning the bronze.

Abrahams was the first European to win this, the most coveted of sprinting honours, and remained the only British athlete to have won it until Allan Wells of Scotland carried it off in 10·25 seconds at the 1980 Moscow Games (a time outside the Olympic and world record of 9·95 seconds). Abrahams said later that he owed it all to Mussabini. 'Under his guidance I managed to improve that decisive one per cent, which made all the difference between supreme success and obscurity.'

In May 1925, Abrahams seriously injured his leg while long-jumping, and he never competed again. But he often remarked on the difference the Olympic medal had made to his life. It gave him the impetus to break into journalism and broadcasting at an early age, and guaranteed him universal respect as he began to climb the administrative ladder of sport. While Liddell was teaching Chinese peasants and diffidently refusing to speak of his Olympic triumph, Abrahams was being appointed to ever higher athletics boards and honestly welcoming the potency of gold. He died in January 1978, a leading and highly esteemed figure in the athletics world.

On Tuesday, 8 July, Liddell cruised through the heats of the 200 metres. Abrahams and William Nichol of Great Britain were also through. On the same day, Douglas Lowe won the 800 metres for Britain in just half a second outside record time.

Wednesday, 9 July, saw Liddell and Abrahams lined up together with four Americans for the final of the 200 metres. It was won by Jackson Scholz in a record 21·6 seconds, with Charles Paddock second. *The Scotsman* informed its readers the next day that Abrahams had been sixth and last; half-way through its description of just how Abrahams had gone about being last ('running like a selling plater', as Abrahams was later to say), it casually offered the additional information that 'Eric Liddell, the Scottish sprinter, scored points for Britain by running into third place'. It notes that he failed to produce his strong finish, and adds: 'He was well placed and had his spurt been forthcoming he would undoubtedly have won.' The fact that Liddell had won a bronze medal for Britain at his first Olympic appearance, and that he was the first Scot ever to win an Olympic medal in the 200 metres, was not brought to the readers' attention.

The immeasurably different status of the Olympic Games then and now is nowhere more gloriously illustrated than in the press coverage of the event. 'Low-key' is the word: 'Liddell scored points for Britain by running into third place . . .' One could meditate for a week without coming up with a more demure way of saying 'Bronze for Britain!' as today's newspapers would shout. And when *The Scotsman*, still playing it all down, eventually announced to the Scottish public that they now had an Olympic world-record quarter-mile champion, the information comes three quarters of the way down its news summary: 'E. H. Liddell, the Edinburgh University sprinter, set up a world's record for the 400 metres at the Olympic Games,' it said, directing attention to page 9 for a full report. On page 9 we find 'Olympic Games, Liddell's Great Victory' sandwiched between 'Nature Notes, Young Hedgehogs and the Cannibal' and 'Liberal Policy, Opponents' Handicaps'. The report itself, though, is lengthy and full of colour.

Incidentally, on 8 July the press reported that Mr Ramsay MacDonald was leaving for Paris for talks with the French Premier. Two days later he had returned to London. Yet no one had linked the Prime Minister's name with the Stade Colombes and the Games or thought fit to comment on the fact that he had been to Paris and had not, even unofficially, visited the stadium for a few minutes to cheer on his compatriots. It speaks volumes about the difference in attitudes to the Olympic Games then and now.

On Thursday, 10 July, Liddell cruised through his first-round heat of the 400 metres in the mediocre time of 50·2, well behind the winner. Later that day he won his quarter-final in a personal best of 49·0. Next day he won his semi-final in 48·2; Liddell was clearly coming into top form at exactly the right moment. His time, however, was slower than that of the American Horatio Fitch, who had just shattered the world and Olympic record in the other semi-final in 47·8, and of the Swiss runner Joseph Imbach, not to mention the gallant Guy Butler who had qualified for the final in a European and UK record of 48·0. There was little to suggest, that Friday afternoon, that Liddell would take world athletics by storm on the same evening.

On the morning of that momentous day, Friday, 11 July, Eric had been handed a note (it was quite an Olympics for little notes of encouragement that would go into the history books). But the one Eric Liddell received was rather different in tone from the message Sam Mussabini had sent to Harold Abrahams, urging him to think of nothing but the pistol and the tape, and run like hell. Liddell's note was much more quixotic, and much better material for legend. It read: 'In the old book it says, "He that honours me I will honour." Wishing you the best of success always.' It was signed by the athletics masseur who attended to Eric and the rest of the British team. The biblical reference he had in mind was 1 Samuel 2, verse 30: 'Them that honour me, I will honour.' He wrote it, as he revealed later, simply because he 'liked Eric so much'.

Eric accepted the note at the Hôtel Moderne in the Rue de la République and said he would read it when he got to the stadium. In the dressing-room after the race he thanked the masseur for the note as he lay on the treatment table. 'I did his left side,' the masseur recalled later, 'and I remember what a great heart he had.' Eric Liddell had that sort of effect on people. There can hardly have been many athletes who moved their masseurs to biblical citations.

The Stade Colombes was baking hot when the six competitors gathered on the track for the 400 metres final. There were two Britons (Liddell and Butler), two Americans (Horatio Fitch and Conrad Taylor), a Swiss (Joseph Imbach) and a Canadian (David Johnson). Liddell went round shaking hands with all his opponents before the start as usual, and his masseur says that he must have been saying good-bye to them because they wouldn't be seeing him again – he would be so far in front. That sounds like hindsight: Liddell had been drawn in the dreaded outside lane – the worst possible place for a relative novice at the event – where he would have to set the pace on his own without knowing how his opponents were faring.

Suddenly there was a blast of pipes and a swirl of kilts. It was the Cameron Highlanders: with a fellow Scot in the final of the 400 metres and a pipe-band only fifty yards away, the temptation had been irresistible. 'Oh, we just wanted to give Liddell a lift,' says General Sir Philip Christison. 'The atmosphere was so light-hearted that I said, "Come on, let's strike up" – and there was nothing the French could do to stop us.' They marched around the arena playing 'The Campbells are Coming'. (Liddell joked to a reporter from the London *Evening Standard* the next day that he suspected either the army general or the British team captain of a dark plot to terrify the opposition!)

At last the stirring strains of the pipes died away. The six finalists settled in their marks and tensed. The pistol cracked, and Eric Liddell in the outside lane was off like a greyhound. People still remember with awe the blistering pace he set in the first half of that incredible race. He flashed past the 200-metre mark at 22·2 seconds – only 0·6 of a second slower than Scholz's winning time in the 200 metres final two days earlier. He was now some three metres clear of his nearest rival, the bandaged Guy Butler, who was making a tremendous effort on the inside.

There was no possibility of Liddell keeping it up, the *aficionados* were thinking in the stands: *no one* could sprint the first 200 metres of a 400-metre race flat out, and stay the pace to the end. He was bound to 'blow up' in the home straight, if not earlier. Besides, there was his ungainly energy-wasting style, arms flailing and knees pumping. (Harold Abrahams was later to say: 'People may shout their heads off about his appalling style. Well, let them. He gets there.')

As the runners came off the bend into the straight (there was only one bend at the Stade Colombes, because the track was 500 metres, which meant the 400-metre track wasn't a full circuit), Fitch was beginning to make up ground. He had overtaken Guy Butler (who would win the bronze) and was now chasing hard after Liddell, who was only two metres ahead of him.

And then the incredible happened. At the moment when any other runner would have started to flag, however determined, Eric Liddell somehow summoned up hidden reserves of strength and stamina. Head back, chin forward, mouth open, knees jumping, arms waving, he put on a spurt and started to *increase* his lead over Fitch. At the tape he was all of five metres ahead, and had won the Olympic title in a world record time of 47·6.

To anyone who knows anything about running, that sensational race was, and still is, almost unbelievable. The time has been bettered, of course, in the inexorable advance of development and technique (the 400 metres at the Moscow Olympics of 1980 was won in 44·60 seconds and the current world record is an awesome 43·86). But it wasn't really the time that mattered; it was the way in which the race had been run, and won.

To give *The Scotsman* its due, its report on the inside pages was unrestrained:

The Union Jack flew in proud majesty over the Colombes Stadium today for the only final down for decision, the 400 metres, which resulted in a great victory for Great Britain. The brilliant running of E. H. Liddell, the Edinburgh University sprinter, was responsible.

There was a gasp of astonishment when Eric Liddell, one of the most popular athletes at Colombes, was seen to be a clear three yards ahead of the field at the half distance. Nearing the tape Fitch and Butler strained every nerve and muscle to overtake him, but could make absolutely no impression on the inspired Scot. With twenty yards to go, Fitch seemed to gain a fraction, but Liddell appeared to sense the American, and with his head back and chin thrust out in his usual style, he flashed past the tape to gain what was probably the greatest victory of the meeting. Certainly there has not been a more popular win. The crowd went into a frenzy of enthusiasm, which was renewed when the loud-speaker announced that once again the world's record had gone by the board.

The Edinburgh *Evening News* was even more ebullient:

All round the banked area, people were on their feet cheering madly, and as if by magic, hosts of Union Jacks appeared above the heads of the raving crowd as Liddell ripped through the tape and into the arms of the Britishers who were waiting for him. For a moment the cheering lasted, then from the loudspeaker came: 'Hello, hello. Winner of the 400 metres: Liddell of Great Britain. The time 47 3/5 is a new world's record.' Again the great roar of cheering went up, and there were long minutes before the announcer could convey that Fitch, of America, was second, and that Butler, who ran second in this event to Rudd, the South African, at Antwerp, was third and Johnson, of Canada, fourth. Thrill followed thrill, for the flags went up, a big Union Jack in the centre, a little one to the left, and a little Stars and Stripes to the right, and again came that hush as all the spectators stood and the bands played. Then came crash upon crash of applause as Liddell walked across the grass and vanished down the stairs to the dressing rooms.

Liddell's time of 47·6 seconds was officially ratified as a world record for the 400 metres. It was not the fastest time in the world, however; the great American runner, Ted Meredith, had earlier recorded 47·4 for the 440 yards, which is more than two metres longer. But Meredith had nothing but praise for Liddell, after watching the race from the stands. He told a reporter that it was the most wonderful quarter-mile that had ever been run. Considering the conditions under which it was run, it was nothing short of marvellous, as Liddell had had to make his own pace from the crack of the pistol to the tape. 'Liddell,' said Meredith, 'is the greatest quarter-miler ever seen.'

Immediately all sorts of people rushed into print to announce that Liddell was a natural quarter-miler and they had always known it. Newspapers which had once called him a 'traitor' now lauded him to the skies, casting off their bland reportage for the occasion. The colour-writers had a field day, as in the Edinburgh *Evening News* feature report:

It was Liddell who first caught the eye as they came round the first bend. The Scot set up a terrific pace. He ran as if he were wild with inspiration, like some demon. And as he flew along to the accompaniment of a roar, the experts wondered whether Liddell would crack, such was the pace he set out to travel. 'Liddell' was shrieked, 'Imbach' was thundered by the Swiss, 'Taylor' was shouted by a finely drilled American clique; 'Butler', 'Fitch' in turn were yelled. Liddell, yards ahead, came round the bend for the straight, and as he did so he pulled the harder at himself, for Fitch was getting nearer. There was Butler too, and Imbach to be reckoned with. It was the last fifty metres that meant the making or breaking of Liddell. Just for a second it was feared that he would kill himself by the terrible speed he had got up, but to the joy of the British camp, he remained chock full of fight. Imbach, perhaps fifty yards from the tape, fell. It was then Liddell or Fitch. The Scotsman had so surely got all his teeth into the race that the American could not hold, and Liddell got home first by what, considering the formidable opposition, was almost a remarkable finish. Butler was third, Johnson next, and then Taylor, who had the bad luck to stumble a yard or two from the finish.

The *Bulletin*, Scotland's popular picture-paper of those days, called Liddell's race 'the greatest achievement in the Olympic Games so far', and went on:

This is the crowning distinction of Liddell's great career on the track, and no more modest or unaffected world champion could be desired. Liddell has built up his success by hard work and perseverance, and although hardly a beautiful runner he has even triumphed over his defects of style.

These 'defects of style' made his win all the more remarkable. 'That lad Liddell's a hell of an awful runner,' Jack Moakley, wisest and oldest of the American team, had remarked the evening before the race, 'but he's got something. I think he's got what it takes.' Nobody could quite define that 'something', and the last person to try was Liddell himself, who was content to tell an interviewer afterwards that he had just 'gone all out'.

Liddell did not stay around for long in the stadium after his race. He had an address to deliver on Sunday at a church service in the old Scots Kirk in Paris for all the Olympic competitors, and he slipped away quietly to prepare it. Behind him, pencils scribbled and wires buzzed and the race was relived on a thousand tongues. Already they were speculating: Would he have won the race he never entered – the 100 metres? It has been asked many times since, and it remains the great unknowable.

But fifty-six years and twelve Olympics later, somebody else, in a curious, fanciful sort of way, ran the 100 metres race for him. A Scotsman won the jewel of the sprint titles at last. And when Allan Wells was asked after the race if he had run it for Harold Abrahams, the British winner from 1924, Wells replied quietly: 'No, this one was for Eric Liddell.'

3

'This Awful Grim Business'

Of course, Eric Liddell would hardly have recognized the kind of Olympic Games that Allan Wells attended in 1980 – 'This awful grim business that passes under the name of sport', as Laurie Liddell, until recently Director of Physical Education at Edinburgh University puts it.

Think of what it's like now. Television cameras rove the stadium, picking out the gigantic electronic scoreboard, the perfect curves and synthetic surface of the running-track, the vast armies of officials and journalists and photographers and security police. Athletes spring past, decked from head to toe in all the sporting equipment necessary to run a perfect race – lightweight running-vest and pants, specially spiked shoes, track-suits, windcheaters. Their bodies are taut, minds concentrated on releasing the fruits of months of training into one magnificent explosion of speed or height or endurance; calves moulded and muscled from mile upon mile of road and track foot-pounding; thighs bulging from agonizing sessions of press-ups and weight-training.

Now and then the name of some commercial sports-equipment firm flashes by, adorning a T-shirt or sports bag. In the radio and television commentators' boxes studded around the stadium the talk is excited . . . To whom is that athlete, Steve Ovett, spelling out 'I-love-you' messages in front of the camera? . . . Is there any truth in the rumour that one of the long-distance runners has just come out of hospital after having had a total blood-change to improve his chances of winning?

And, dominating all discussion, is the question of politics. Have the Games become merely a platform for political expression and pressure? Can sportsmen and sportswomen separate their personal commitment to sport from political and national loyalties? What's happened to the ideals of peace and unity through sport?

What would Eric Liddell have made of it all today? It's a far cry from his world of cinder tracks and digging starting-holes with a trowel – and shaking hands with all your opponents before a race.

Willie Carmichael, a vice-president of the SAAA and organizer of the 1970 Commonwealth Games in Edinburgh, roars with laughter at the very thought of it – Eric Liddell would certainly have to make some changes if he appeared at a sports meeting today. Carmichael picks up an old picture of Eric posing with some running mates and stabs it gleefully with his finger:

'Look at his long pants and his short sleeves! Nobody wears that today. They wear things like bathing trunks and short pants. And look at him in this picture. He's standing there in his blazer, freezing. They just didn't have tracksuits in those days – or anything fancy like that.'

However, the relatively minor question of attire wouldn't be the only problem to confront Eric. His attitudes, his expectations . . . in fact his whole way of life would have to undergo a revolution. And, according to Tom Riddell, the former Scottish champion miler who ran with Eric in the old days, Eric would not have appreciated many of the aspects of this new style.

'Eric would turn in his grave if he saw the way today's athletes run around with the name of commercial advertisers emblazoned on all their gear. He'd have been appalled at the sight of "amateurs" running for money. And as for those fellows who do a lap of honour after winning a race . . .!'

And Professor Neil Campbell, a fellow-runner at Edinburgh University in the 1920s, thinks that even with all the opportunities that the 'sophisticated' techniques of sport today have to offer, Eric would, quite simply, not have been prepared to take advantage of them.

'If he was around today? He'd still have been a splendid runner, but I don't think he'd have been able to participate in all the big championships here, there and everywhere. I just don't think he would have done it. You see, training in those days wasn't anything like what we do now. A seven-day-week training session was just not on for him. He had his studies and other commitments. His training was fairly intensive – but only two or three times a week. There was nothing like the fantastic dedication of today – that just wasn't on. Eric's studies – although he wasn't a particularly great student – were all-important to him. He had to get a degree, and that was important to him. Running was important – he got a great deal of pleasure out of it – but it took second place.'

The kind of dedication which puts sport in only second place just isn't good enough today if you want to be a top athlete. Scotland's Allan Wells won the 100 metres at the 1980 Olympics in Moscow, but it cost him a lot!

'Training twice a day, seven days a week, is the only way I can do it,' he says.

His life is totally dominated by rigorous training sessions: work-outs in the gym, weightlifting, press-ups, working at the punch-ball ('We count each punch on the ball to alleviate some of the boredom, but it can be a strain'); practising that explosive start from the blocks a thousand times over; running round the track again and again – 4×60 metres . . . 4×80 metres . . . 4×100 metres. And the miles and miles of jogging through rain and snow or in uncomfortable heat. Golfing, cycling and all the other sports he enjoys are banned during his work-up to a race, because they develop the wrong muscles and would spoil his running.

Wells's training is intensive, but not unusual for an athlete today. 'My sacrifices for sport are no different and no greater than any other athlete's. We've all got to give up something.'

Linsey Macdonald, winner of a bronze medal in the 1980 Olympics 4×400 metres relay, is only fifteen and still at school.

Yet she trains two hours every evening from Monday to Thursday, and three hours on Sunday afternoons.

'It's hard training, and it's quite difficult to do homework as well, but if you do have a success it's worth it.'

This sort of intensive training isn't a new development in sport. Back in the late 1960s, the 400 metres hurdler David Hemery was undertaking a gruelling non-stop sixty-week build-up for the 1968 Olympics at Mexico City, where he won the final by the huge margin of seven metres and lopped seven tenths of a second off the previous world record.

It might even be argued that Harold Abrahams, who is said to have been the first British athlete to have a personal coach (Sam Mussabini), was right in there at the beginnning of this trend: he was learning all about shortened strides and 'drop-finishes' while Liddell was wobbling down the track with his arms flailing like windmills.

If given the chance now, Eric would probably have been delighted to lose his 'wobble' and enjoy all the other benefits that modern training has to offer. He loved a challenge and he exulted in feeling that, when he ran, he was putting every scrap of his ability into that race. He was far too much of a competitor not to be intrigued by the possibilities that today's sporting techniques offer the athlete: the opportunity of running even faster. However, what would have concerned Eric, and would probably have discouraged him from entering the world of top athletics, would be the way that the pursuit of athletic excellence today consumes the life of the athlete so totally. Allan Wells hits the nail on the head when he says, 'We've all got to give up something.' That 'something', in Liddell's case, would have had to be his spiritual commitments.

Ron Pickering, sports commentator, coach and former athlete, agrees.

'In Eric Liddell's time, training was not so exacting that he couldn't think of higher things, academically and spiritually; whereas now if athletes are planning to enter the ministry they wait until later in their career. No athlete today could go and train two or three times a week and get away with it. In Liddell's day, it was merely par for the course. The demands, in terms of time, mean that athletes now have to change their lifestyle, to ration their time. If, for example, an athlete wants to go to university, then he'll have to take four, five, even six years to do a three- or four-year course. It's damn difficult, if you are a coal-miner, to be an athlete today, and impossible to be a swimmer or a gymnast. Sport today isn't just different from the 1920s – it's different from sport twenty years ago. It's difficult to contemplate the world's greatest miler wanting to be a surgeon today – but that's what Roger Bannister had his sights set on.'

So Eric Liddell would have had to choose between a career in sport or a career as a missionary – and that would have been no choice at all in Liddell's eyes. He might also have decided that sport today is just too serious a business to be worth considering. Eric ran to win, but he also ran because he enjoyed it. And as Laurie Liddell (no relation) says 'enjoyment' is hardly a word that is overused in descriptions of top-level sport today.

'I think that a great deal of the joy has gone out of sport today. It has ceased to be *play* – it's just jolly hard work to stay at the top level in modern sport. I wonder occasionally if we're getting our priorities a little wrong; I really think that we're getting to the stage now where we've got to ask where the demarcation line is between what used to be this lovely, enjoyable activity that we all could take part in – and this awful, grim business now that passes under the name of sport.

'Must we measure "progress" in the athletics sense of "higher", "faster", "further" all the time? Questions are being asked like – what is the ultimate of man's performance? And even, what do we mean today by man and woman? By the time we've got around to techniques of changing blood and things of that sort to improve athletic performance – once we begin to indulge in almost a form of spare-part surgery – I think the question has really got to be asked: where do we stop and still preserve something of what we might call athletics, or indeed sport in general?'

An 'awful grim business'. It's a cry from the heart of so many of those former athletes and trainers from Eric's time. A despair for the future of sport. A yearning for the good old days of true dedicated amateurism.

Allan Wells says frankly. 'I don't want to say that running is like a job – but it is almost a profession now.'

But had it not been going that way already, even in the 1920s when Eric Liddell was electrifying the athletics world? Think back to the very first modern Olympic Games, held in Athens in 1896, and think of all the developments and innovations which had taken place by the time of the Paris Olympics in 1924.

In 1896 only thirteen nations were represented and only nine sports were on the programme: cycling, fencing, gymnastics, lawn tennis, shooting, swimming, track and field athletics, weight-lifting, and wrestling. The Games were so informal then that a British lawn tennis player entered the Olympic tournament simply in order to secure a court to play on, because the courts were in the Olympic stadium. And several of the 500 entries were inquisitive tourists visiting Athens for the first time, and eager to share in all the new experiences on offer! By the time of the Third Olympics at St Louis in 1904, there were twenty-five competitions and a suspiciously fresh-looking marathon runner called Fred Lorz won the race by fifteen minutes, but was disqualified when it was revealed that he had hitched a lift for ten miles of the course in a truck! Those were the days!

The 1912 Games in Stockholm saw an important development when, for the first time, a country – Sweden, the host country – employed a professional coach to prepare its Olympic team. Within two years Britain and Germany had their own national coaches, but the First World War meant that there were no Berlin Games in 1916 at which the athletes could show off the fruits of their professional preparation. This sort of professional coaching was then abandoned until twenty years later, at the next Berlin Games in 1936; but the tendency had been born.

By the Paris Olympics of 1924 the Games were no longer recognizable as the same cosy occasion launched by the Hellenic Olympic Committee in Athens on Easter Sunday in 1896. In those days, the 311 athletes who attended all came to Athens on their own initiative and at their own expense. By 1924 there were subsidized national teams – a form of sponsored nationalism. Perhaps the Olympic Games were never really what the original idealists had hoped they would be.

For many years the Games were attended by only a tiny minority of the world's nations and athletes. The Third World hardly got a look-in, while the huge but socially backward nations of Russia and China had too many problems on their hands to be seriously concerned with a mere athletics competition. The United States and Western Europe dominated the Games, and even then it was only a fraction of the populations of these countries who had the opportunity to compete. For instance, in the 1924 Olympics in Paris, almost 20 per cent of the British team were attending the universities of Oxford or Cambridge at the time.

At a time when women were fighting tooth and nail in many parts of the Western world for social and political rights, it's not surprising to learn that the Olympics were all-male affairs for the first thirty years of their existence. The breakthrough came in 1928 when women were allowed to enter for the Amsterdam Games. There was, admittedly, a somewhat modest programme – only five events; but a start had been made, and world records were produced at each of the events. This victory for women suffered a setback, however, over the 800 metres, when, because of the distress shown by several of the finalists, the race was dropped from the Olympic Calendar and not reinstated in the women's programme until 1960.

Since the Second World War there have been tremendous developments. At Helsinki in 1952 the USSR entered the Games for the first time and began to show its formidable potential, with its team performing well in the men's events and dominating the women's events. As one sports writer, Tom McNab, has put it in *The Complete Book of Athletics*: '. . . in the 1952–60 period more was discovered about athletics techniques and training methods than had been unearthed in the previous two thousand years.'

Technological changes have been enormous as well. Until 1964, cinder or clay tracks were used at all the Olympic Games and other major championships. However, by the time of the Mexico Games in 1968 the Tartan track – a synthetic resin surface patented in the USA and originally designed for horse racing – had been generally accepted as the best all-round track both as regards performance in all weathers and ease of maintenance. Starting-blocks, although invented in 1927, only came into general use after the Second World War, so that a trowel was no longer an essential part of an athlete's sports equipment. Since 1964, the official timing of competitors at the Olympics has been provided by photo-finish devices. Other developments might not be regarded as being quite so healthy for sport. Tom McNab wrote:

The 1960 Games were the first to be televised on a world basis, and it was the increasing demand for televised sport which was to transform athletics in the Western world. Television attracted attention, and attention attracted sponsors. Increased state aid in the East, and an increase in sponsorship money and sports scholarships in the West, have increasingly made the term 'amateur' irrelevant and meaningless . . . There is therefore no way in which the world's best athletes can any longer be called amateurs, for they receive directly, or in kind, more help than is required to pursue their sport . . . This is the natural result of increased state, public, and commercial interest in the sport, but it has created a generation of dishonest athletes.

The trend which has caused the greatest concern among lovers of 'fair' sport, however, is the growth of the use of drugs by athletes over the last two decades – drugs such as anabolic steroids to stimulate the work-rate of an athlete. According to Rule 144 of the International Amateur Athletics Federation's regulations, 'Doping is the employment of drugs with the intention of increasing athletic efficiency by their stimulating action upon muscles or nerves, or by paralysing the sense of fatigue. Their use is strongly deprecated not only on moral grounds but also because of their danger to health.' The rule further states that athletes must submit to an anti-dope test if required to do so by the organizers of a meeting.

And although Rule 141(3) of the IAAF's regulations lays down that 'All women's entries must be accompanied by a certificate as to sex, issued by a qualified medical doctor . . .', by 1966 it was found necessary to require women at major international competitions to undergo a sex-determination test.

Drugs? Sex-determination tests? Eric Liddell might very well not have been impressed with modern sport. But perhaps the sports world wouldn't have been particularly impressed with Eric Liddell, either – in a professional sense. Tom McNab, a British National Athletics Coach from 1963 to 1977, puts Liddell into the perspective of modern athletics: 'Yes, Eric would have been a great runner – maybe even made the finals of the Olympics – but I don't think he'd win an Olympic title nowadays. You see, Eric was only 5 feet 9 inches . . . He would be limited by his size. And his potential would definitely have been in the 100 metres, not the 400.'

So Eric, according to Tom McNab, would not have been the Superman of the 1980s. And McNab knows all about Eric Liddell: he won the Eric Liddell Memorial Cup for the best junior athlete in Scotland, way back in 1952. And he has also been involved in the *Chariots of Fire* film, coaching the actors in how to run. He couldn't help but become interested in Eric Liddell: 'I had to teach Ian Charleson how to run . . . and then I had to train him how to run badly.' Eric Liddell intrigues him – 'God in action', is how he describes him. And he admits that Eric's running times are 'remarkable' for the amount of training he did. Nevertheless, he insists that Eric's achievements should be put in perspective.

'You see, in those days very few people ran. They usually went to university, which meant that the majority of them were from middle-class backgrounds.' Even twenty years ago it was the same. He recalls the story of when Jimmy Reid, the Clydeside 'voice of the workers' heard the news that Roger Bannister had broken the four-minute mile in 1954. Apparently, during a meeting down at the Clydeside dockyards, he held up a pair of spiked running-shoes and asked the men how many of them owned a pair themselves. No one put up his hand.

It was easy enough for an Oxford student to be a great runner, if he had the ability; but what about the people who never got the chance to find out if they could run at all?

McNab believes that sport is far more democratic nowadays. Many more people are involved, from the top level right down to the 'popular' level. He also points out that it's only in the last decade or so that athletes of the huge Communist bloc have entered, and increasingly dominated, the sporting world.

No, Eric Liddell was very much a 'man of his times' and it's probably pointless to try to transpose him into a world in which the conditions and opportunities are so totally different. 'Sport was very much a recreation in those days,' says Tom McNab. 'And Eric Liddell reflected that attitude. What he was doing then was much more cavalier, much more fun than the attitude today. The fun is still there – at the bottom level, where more and more people have the chance to enjoy themselves. Look at the number of people who play squash nowadays. It's at the top that it's a lot less fun. The training's hard and there's a lot of pressure (although I'd call it more a form of pleasure, not pressure, because to succeed is so pleasurable). No, it's not fun, but then it's like the difference between going to the theatre and seeing a farce or a Shakespearian tragedy – the farce is fun, the tragedy isn't, but they both give immense pleasure.'

McNab realizes that there is much that is wrong in sport today: 'Never again will there be what we would call a "fair" competition. For instance, I would find it very difficult nowadays to single out a runner from the final of any of the Olympic races I could be sure hadn't taken drugs. Now that just couldn't have happened at the 1924 Olympics. The forces of evil are much better organized today.'

Does he think that sport and the Olympic ideal need a man like Liddell to bring sanity and principle back into play? 'Well, firstly, I don't think we could have an Eric Liddell in the 1980s – the values of the 1920s would be totally out of place. But people do still make a stand on principle, you know. A lot of people refused to go to the Moscow Olympics – that was a moral stand. But you didn't hear about them because their names weren't big enough.'

McNab is a hard-headed realist. Yes, he regrets some of the 'unhealthy' influences in sport today. But he is too aware of the advantages that progress has brought to want to turn the clock back. The world of amateur athletics – of cavalierism and Eric Liddell – he consigns to the nineteenth century: 'They have no place in the twentieth century. Professionalism

66

is here to stay . . . It's just a matter of admitting it, of getting rid of the hypocrisy.'

Yet there are those who believe that sport is now being engulfed by that very hypocrisy and by other vices – by violence, excessive professionalism, drugs, secret handouts, deceit.

Ron Pickering is outspoken: 'Sport has to be a sanctuary. It has to be something bigger than everyday life and have something to look up to. That's why values are so important and why we keep the Olympic torch burning even when people want to extinguish it.'

Is he trying to turn the clock back? He agrees that there is a tide he would like to stem: 'I want sport to be more honest. I want us to re-examine the rules and the laws. There is no way I can support hypocrisy. Sport has to be handed back to teachers and philosophers and taken out of the hands of entrepreneurs and chemists.'

Could we do with an Eric Liddell today?

'Sure. We are desperately short of characters and personalities. It really doesn't matter whether they are highly religious. We really need the characters of which *Boys' Own* stories are made.'

And what about the athletes themselves? It's all very well bemoaning the fate of sport and the loss of something very special; but in the end it's the athlete who counts. Even allowing for the fact that sport is a much more serious business than it used to be in Eric Liddell's day, a great deal of pleasure is derived from it. Why else would thousands of men and women put themselves through the gruelling training? There must be something more.

The Olympic champion hurdler Davie Hemery, who is the head track and field coach at Boston University, believes that he can quite easily reconcile his own quiet Christian faith with his commitment to top-level athletics: 'You see, to do one's best, to get the most out of oneself athletically – that can be a spiritual experience. I don't think we should look back. But there needs to be a bit of re-education as to what sport can be in terms of personal growth. Sport still holds quite a lot that is intrinsically good and worth while. People can discover themselves and a purpose to life. Sport doesn't need to be the sole aspect of one's life – but it can be an important tool. At certain times sport can be the most important tool of all.'

Allan Wells comments: 'There's a lot of pressure, but it sort of gets a hold of you. It's something I still enjoy, because it's learning about yourself, and believing you can do it.'

But wouldn't he like to be back in the days of the gentleman amateur?   To which he replies: 'Look here, I *am* a gentleman amateur.'

Like Eric Liddell.

4

'None Can Pass You But the Examiner'

As Eric Liddell prepared for his journey home from the Paris Olympics, two university dons in Edinburgh were hatching a plot over a cup of Sunday-afternoon tea. One was the professor of Greek, Dr Mair; the other was responsible for the graduation ceremony that was to take place on Thursday, 17 July, five days ahead. One of the graduands would be Eric Liddell, the hero of the Olympics, and the students would be expecting something rather special to mark the occasion. What could be done?

They approached the keeper of the Royal Botanic Garden in Edinburgh. Did he have anything in the way of wild olive leaves, by any chance? The keeper thought he could manage something – oleaster, perhaps, a garden derivative of the wild olive.

So the plans were laid. There would be not just a graduation ceremony but a crowning ceremony as well. The professor of Greek sat down with pen and dictionary and composed an elegant encomium in Greek. The principal and vice-chancellor of the university, Sir Alfred Ewing, responded to the whole idea with great enthusiasm; and, on 17 July 1924, *The Scotsman* duly informed its readers that a rather special graduation ceremony was to take place at Edinburgh University that day: Eric Liddell was to be crowned with an olive wreath in honour of his Olympic victory.

The domed McEwan Hall in Edinburgh, donated to the

university by the brewery family, had been for years the venue for graduations and degree examinations. Over the years, successive generations of students had sat in their serried ranks waiting to be 'capped', or letting their eyes wander over its magnificent decorations in a desperate search for exam inspiration. In the dome, fifteen figures representing the Arts and Sciences, painted against a background of gold to create the effect of an enamelled jewel; and a suitably edifying inscription: 'Wisdom is the principal thing; therefore get wisdom; and with all thy getting, get understanding. Exalt her, and she shall bring thee honour.' Over the top of the imposing platform, and on either side of it, they could gaze at huge fresco panels: Minerva, as the tutelary deity of the university, seated upon a marble throne in the Grove of Academia, receiving the gift of the building itself, with the donor modestly lurking in the group of figures to her left; the Temple of Fame, showing nearly a hundred assorted philosophers and students attending a triple throne occupied by the three goddesses representing Science, Art and Literature; and a panel depicting 'Fame crowning Success'.

Never had the McEwan Hall decorations seen a more appropriate occasion: Fame had indeed crowned Success, and Edinburgh University was not going to let anyone forget it. There were several distinguished honorary graduands present that morning to receive their degrees – people like G. M. Trevelyan, the historian, Lord Macmillan, Sir Frederick Whyte, Mrs Sidney Webb, the economist and sociologist, and Sir Owen Seaman, the editor of *Punch*. But none of them had any illusions: this was going to be Eric Liddell's day, not theirs.

It was quite apparent [*The Scotsman* reported the following morning] that those present had been reserving themselves to greet the Olympic victor. As Mr Liddell stepped forward to receive the ordinary degree of Bachelor of Science, the vast audience rose and cheered him to the echo. The cheering continued for an appreciable time and there were several calls for silence before Sir Alfred Ewing could make himself heard.

When the principal and vice-chancellor eventually managed to get a hearing, he produced the *bon mot* he must have been sweating over for days, and which has now been immortalized in the Liddell legend.

'Mr Liddell,' he said, 'you have shown that none can pass you but the examiner . . .

'In the ancient Olympic tests the victor was crowned with wild olive by the high priest of Zeus, and a poem written in his honour was presented to him. A vice-chancellor is no high priest, but he speaks and acts for the university; and in the name of the university, to which you have brought fresh honour, I present you with this epigram in Greek, composed by Professor Mair, and place upon your head this chaplet of wild olive.'

The cheering now knew no bounds. As the wreath was placed on his lowered head, the Greek scroll containing the fruits of Professor Mair's labours was put in his hand. It was probably unintelligible to Liddell himself, who had studied science, not the humanities. Translated, it read:

> Happy the man who the wreathed games essaying
>> Returns with laurelled brow,
> Thrice happy victor thou, such speed displaying
>> As none hath showed till now;
>> We joy, and Alma Mater, for thy merit
>> Proffers to thee this crown:
>> Take it, Olympic Victor. While you wear it
>> May Heaven never frown.

Outside the McEwan Hall, the students grabbed Eric and carried him in a sedan-chair on their shoulders along the Edinburgh streets to St Giles Cathedral, where the traditional graduation service was to be held. In the newspaper photographs of Eric Liddell that day he was clearly enjoying himself, perched up there in his gown and hood on the victory chair, scroll in hand, wreath on head and enormous grin all over his face.

The photographs say a lot about Eric Liddell. Yes, he was modest. Yes, he slipped away from the Olympic arena to pray after his race, instead of joining the victory party. Yes, he wore his ordinary old suit to the dinner in his honour because it didn't occur to him to wear anything else. But there was not a scrap of

71

pious asceticism in him. In the photographs you don't see a man who is enjoying the attention but trying to pretend that he's not; or a man whose mind is perforce on loftier things than a noisy student carnival, or who is embarrassed at being up here when earthly glory, as the preacher always saith, is vanity. Eric Liddell is quite simply enjoying himself. He knew how to savour life.

By the time they reached the steps of St Giles, the medieval church whose stones have witnessed so much of Scotland's history, another crowd had gathered, and a speech was called for.

Eric Liddell talked to them about the words inscribed over the gate of Pennsylvania University: 'In the dust of defeat as well as in the laurels of victory there is a glory to be found if one has done his best.' Those who had done their best and failed to win the laurels, said Eric, were owed as much honour as those who received them.

Sir Richard Lodge, the historian, said at the graduation lunch that he could not remember so much of the ancient Greek spirit about Edinburgh as he had noted that day, and proposed a toast to 'Our Olympic victor'. Eric's reply made them laugh. He said that he was a short-distance runner owing to a defect in his constitution. He was extremely short-winded and therefore he would not keep them long. He blamed his unorthodox running style on his ancestors, who as Scottish Borderers were wont to make the odd foray into England and return rather faster than they went. That capacity for speed seemed to have been handed down from generation to generation, he said, and nobody looked for stylishness in a returning raider!

He ended by reminding them that a man was composed of three parts: body, mind and soul, and it was only when they educated each part in harmony that they would get the best and truest graduates from the university.

At the end of the lunch, a team of university 'Blues' drew up in a carriage. Eric and the principal were invited inside, and off they went, escorted by hundreds of students from all the faculties. With Eric still wearing his olive wreath, the procession toured the city. They trooped along the historic Royal Mile and down to Princes Street, Edinburgh's main throroughfare. As crowds milled around them the police themselves entered into the spirit of the proceedings, and allowed the carriage on to the pavement.

They ended up outside the principal's house, where yet another crowd had materialized. Before they all went in for tea, Sir Alfred Ewing told the audience with a chuckle that he had never in his life basked in so much reflected glory in one day.

But the Olympic celebrations still had plenty of mileage in them. The next day poor Eric had to sit through another series of eulogies at a public dinner in his honour. He may have enjoyed the fun of being carted round by his fellow-students, but listening to glowing tributes was something he always found hard to bear. Dr Norman Maclean of St Cuthbert's Parish Church in Edinburgh described in *The Scotsman* Liddell's reply to the speeches made in his honour at that dinner.

'It was a difficult task amid that enthusiasm. The shouting and the cheering suddenly ceased, and he began to speak. The modesty and simplicity and directness of his words went straight to the heart. No adulation, no fame, no flattery can ever affect this youth with the clean-cut features, the level eyes, and the soft voice. He has got that great redeeming gift, the gift of humour . . . He made us quickly realize that running was not to be his career. He was training to be a missionary in China, and he was to devote all his spare time until he set forth for the East in evangelistic work among the young men in Scotland.

'What a hush suddenly fell,' continued Dr Maclean, who was beginning to enjoy himself and add a touch of purple to the picture. 'The Olympic Games were forgotten; the olive crowns and the thunder of the cheers; and we saw this young man go forth on his mission . . .'

You are spared the tributes that emanated from the Lord Provost's complimentary luncheon the next week, though no one spared Eric. But this column from the Edinburgh University undergraduate magazine, the *Student*, is worth noting as a record of the opinion of at least some of his peers:

Success in athletics sufficient to turn the head of any ordinary man, has left Liddell absolutely unspoilt, and his modesty is entirely genuine and unaffected. He has taken his triumphs in his stride, as it were, and has never made any sort of fuss. What he has thought it right to do, that he has done, looking neither to the left nor to the right, and yielding not one jot or tittle of principle either to court applause or to placate criticism. Courteous and affable, he is utterly free from 'gush'. Devoted to his principles, he is without a touch of Pharisaism. The best that can be said of any student is that he has left the fame of his university fairer than he found it, and his grateful Alma Mater is proud to recognize that to no man does that praise more certainly belong than to Eric Henry Liddell.

In London, still just a few days after his Olympic triumph, Eric Liddell showed once and for all that his glorious running in Paris had been no fluke. In the British Empire v. USA contest he ran the final leg of the 4×440 yards relay race in a time that was reckoned to be under 48 seconds – and possibly as low as 46 seconds. He started the leg about five yards behind his old American rival, Horatio Fitch, and beat him by a stride. It was an outstanding race.

A year later he carried off his last athletics appearance in Scotland with all his usual flair. It was described afterwards by Professor Neil Campbell as a performance 'of uninterrupted triumph'. A crowd of 12,000 were at the Scottish Amateur Athletics Association meeting at Hampden Park in Glasgow in June to see him equal his own Scottish record time of 10·0 seconds in the 100 yards. They also watched him storm home in 22·2 seconds in the 220, and in 49·2 seconds in the 440 yards (these were also both best Championship performances). It was the first time that fifty seconds had been broken at the Scottish Championships, and the feat was not to be repeated until 1937 or bettered until 1957.

Liddell was only the fourth athlete ever to have won the three short races together at the SAAA. The Jamaican Scot Alf Downer managed it three times in 1893, 1894 and 1895 before turning professional; Hugh Welsh, essentially a miler, and Wyndham Halswelle, the man who won Britain's first Olympic gold for the 400 metres in 1908, achieved the three Scottish titles in 1906. Liddell achieved it twice at Hampden Park, in 1924 and again in 1925. And on this second occasion he was also a member of the winning relay team.

That was Liddell's last Scottish appearance in the summer of

1925, but there was plenty of leg-work in him yet – as the Chinese would soon be finding out. Eric had set his mind, years earlier, on going back to China as a missionary. He had been born there, and maybe there was something of the spirit of the place in his blood, perhaps even a trace of the ancient language silent on his tongue. China can take hold of you that way. Besides, his parents were there, his sister was there, his elder brother Rob had gone back there as a medical missionary. He wanted to spend his life sharing his faith, and so he turned, like them, to China.

Here again in Eric's life there was none of the obvious heart-searching that the story-teller is always hunting for. There seems to have been no soliloquy on the lure of stardom and how difficult it was to tear himself away; no dark night of the soul, no dream with beckoning Chinese figures, no missionary call that changed his life, no verse from Isaiah – not even a note from D. P. Thomson, who is usually so helpful, to record a climactic moment when Eric might have come up to him and said, 'I'm going to China. I decided last night.'

Eric just always seems to have known that this was what he would do. He kept his studies up at university – though he was hardly a born academic – because he knew he needed a degree to be useful as a teacher in China. And when he returned from the Olympics in 1924, he enrolled at the Scottish Congregational College in Edinburgh so that he would have a theological qualification under his belt, too. The Anglo-Chinese College in Tientsin, to which he had been provisionally appointed, wanted him to share in the religious work as well as teach science and supervise athletics.

5

'It Was the Beatle-mania of the Day'

Eric Liddell spent his last year in Scotland studying divinity at the Scottish Congregational College in Edinburgh. The Congregational Church, in which he had been brought up, is doctrinally similar to the Church of Scotland, but the whole congregation participates in church government, instead of delegating authority through the presbytery system.

It was a hectic year for him. In addition to attending classes, much of his time was spent far from the college – in theatres, music halls, churches, schools, auditoriums and other colleges all over Scotland and occasionally in England. This was the year in which he became fully associated with the student evangelistic campaigns.

These student campaigns were a phenomenon of the 1920s which left a deep mark on the religious life of Scotland. It is difficult nowadays to imagine what it was like in the days when the minutiae of church affairs were splashed – or at least liberally sprinkled – over the newspapers every day. There were reports of Mission to Lepers meetings, and missionary federations, and every conceivable church society. The churches' loud demands for stricter drinking laws constantly dominated the headlines. Churchmen's views were sought as avidly as trade-union leaders are courted by the media today.

It is just as difficult to visualize the impact of a handful of students who in 1922 started touring the country at week-ends, trying to inject some life into the staid Scottish Kirk. Just imagine a newspaper report today like this one from the *Ardrossan and Saltcoats Herald* in September 1924:

Several students from Glasgow University are in Ardrossan this week conducting an evangelistic campaign, and consequently we are hearing fresh voices, if not a new Gospel. Whether staid and respectable church-going folk are disposed to agree with all the methods of the students or not, we think that such campaigns are needed in these days.

In another issue the same paper enthused:

Their theme is familiar enough, but they have come with fresh enthusiasm to present it in their way and from their own angle. They preach a strong, virile message, related to the needs and problems of the day, which they believe to be essential to right the wrongs and transform the life of individuals and society.

The *Airdrie and Coatbridge Advertiser* was much impressed by the numbers who flocked to the mass meetings and much uplifted by the spectacle of the local church being filled every evening of the week with 'an eager and expectant congregation'. And a columnist in one of the Wishaw papers was full of admiration for the rippling muscles of these young Apollos.

The students [he said] are a group of eager, alert, bustling, athletic and well-developed young men, full of enthusiasm and the strength of their own convictions, talking in a manner confident and inspiring, to people many years their seniors, yet with a wonderful power of appeal and magnetic attraction. Far from being kill-joys or milk-sops, these lads represent all that is manly and upright.

The leader of the band was our old friend D. P. Thomson. Back in 1921 Thomson had been present at a Seamen's Mission in Fraserburgh, a fishing town on Scotland's north-east coast, which was sending out signals of 'something happening' in the Church. Reports tell of one meeting where the church was so crammed that young men invaded the pulpit steps to hear the message.

It was their experience in this Fraserburgh Revival that led D. P. Thomson and friends to launch the Glasgow Students' Evangelistic Union (GSEU), perhaps the most vital force in evangelism in the 1920s. Walking down the main street of a Scottish town in these days, you would be sure to meet a notice like this somewhere along the way:

CAMPAIGN FORTNIGHT IN KILMARNOCK
September 20 – October 5
Keep these dates free.
WHY?   WHAT'S ON?
The students are coming!!!

WHERE FROM?   GLASGOW,   EDINBURGH
and St Andrews – the Universities
and the Colleges

WHAT FOR?   WAIT AND SEE!

If there was a special meeting in the campaign, you might find the words in bold capitals: SPEAKER: MR ERIC H. LIDDELL, OLYMPIC ATHLETE. Eric had been taking part in these campaigns ever since the meeting at Armadale in April 1923. He and D. P. would address Glasgow schoolboys and Tyneside men's associations, church women's groups and, on one occasion, the imbibing customers of a Sunday hostelry.

Eric was studying during the day and dashing off every evening and all week-end either to the running-track or to speak in some obscure church hall. He could never say no. His style of oratory remained as flat as ever, and its effect just as mysteriously potent. He continued to tell his young audiences simple stories, parables almost, illustrations garnered from the chemistry lab, the rugby pitch and the running-track. They continued to follow him.

'I think it was just a very simple Christian message,' says Mrs Elsa Watson, who as young Elsa McKechnie was busy planning to set up his fan club around this time. 'There was no difficult theology to understand. All that he said, as far as I can remember, I could write on the back of a post-card.

'I understood what he was talking about – and invariably in churches I have not understood what ministers are talking about.

He talked about what you are going to do tomorrow, and what you are thinking today, and his honesty was just flashing out there the whole time.'

Eric became the president of the Edinburgh branch of the GSEU in the spring of 1925. By this time the 'Manhood Campaigns', as they were called, were in full swing. It sounds faintly suspect today, but the idea of these was to show young men that you didn't need to be a mummy's boy to be a Christian. Eric Liddell – handsome, manly, athletic, blue-eyed Eric – was a godsend to the movement. 'Muscular Christianity' was the phrase on everyone's lips.

'Playing the game of life in a manly and Christian way,' was how the *Glasgow Herald* described one student team's message in a campaign in Barrhead, Renfrewshire.

Their leader, Eric Liddell, has struck that note in all his addresses. He stands for the Christian youth with a clean breeze about him, and his lungs well filled with the air that blows from the Judaean hills. There is not a tincture of conventional piety about any of them; they are interesting and winning. We wish them all the best kinds of success and a closing service that will crown their eight-day effort.

What Eric and his Judaean lungs thought about that encomium is not recorded. Nor his reaction to a poem in another of the local newspapers, believed to have been penned by an adoring daughter of the manse.

ERIC LIDDELL!

To Barrhead comes a gallant man,
   Who in Olympic races ran,
Gained first prize, and led the van –
   Victorious Eric Liddell!

He comes a nobler race to run,
   To strive for Master's prize – 'Well done,'
Which he'll deserve when duly won –
   Undaunted Eric Liddell!

True soldier of the Cross thou art,
   To fight 'gainst wrong, and take the part

Of sinners struck by Satan's dart –
Great-hearted Eric Liddell!

Eric Liddell had practice enough in deflecting the arrows of hero-worship which came hurtling at him wherever he went. And it wasn't just daughters of the manse firing them off. Elsa McKechnie, who must take the prize for sheer dedication to the job, was a good deal less interested in Liddell's muscular Christianity than his muscular arms – and his twinkling eyes and his dimple and his kind smile and his springy walk. 'It was the Beatle-mania of the day,' she now says.

Elsa was fourteen when she first came across Eric Liddell at Morningside Congregational Church in Edinburgh. 'I remember hearing him and seeing him and thinking that this was someone worth doing something about. I went to some of his meetings and then I decided to form an Eric Liddell Club.' Nearly sixty years later, Elsa McKechnie, now Mrs Watson, can produce with a flourish the rules of the club, whose membership comprised all her best friends at George Watson's Ladies' College. The piece of paper from a school exercise-book announced, in the neatest of schoolgirl scripts, the following:

(1) Each member is entitled to one page of this book, in which a poem, or account of ERIC LIDDELL must be inserted, which must be approved of by the committee.
(2) Before becoming a member of this club, the person in question must undergo an oral examination, put by the founder.
(3) Each member must promise three things. i) Always to uphold ERIC LIDDELL. ii) To attend all meetings arranged by the committee. iii) To keep all rules of the club. It is also desirable that members should use the ERIC LIDDELL line.
(4) Members will be presented with a photo of ERIC LIDDELL, and must promise to put it in a place of honour.
(5) Should any member of this club, do anything unworthy of the club, the committee will at once expel the member in question.

BY ORDER

The object of all this fervour wrote back from his new post in Tientsin on 17 December 1925 to acknowledge the founding of the club. 'I do not know what I might be let in for!!!' wrote Eric in his polite, rather awkward style, peppered as always with triple exclamation marks. 'However, there are times when we have to risk a little and after due consideration I have decided to accept the honour you have given me. You will find my name signed and the date on a piece of paper enclosed.'

Before he left for China, Elsa had dogged him faithfully around Edinburgh and one day plucked up the courage to invite him to tea. 'I asked off early from school and cycled home at top speed. I think my family were all hugely amused. But he came, which was so typical of him – to be kind and considerate to a youngster. I don't think I ate or drank a thing. After he went away I got his teacup and I emptied all the tea leaves into an envelope and put it into an album I kept. I also remember keeping the paper and string of a parcel he sent me. I think Eric looked on it all in a very kindly way, as he did with everything. I think he probably understood.'

He did. He answered all her letters, patiently and formally, in his neat, carefully formed handwriting.

> YMCA c/o Sutties,
> 26 Bedford Place,
> London,
> 22.iv.25

Dear Elsa,

It was so good of you to send me that Easter card also the two p.c.'s. I'm awfully glad you are enjoying your time at Biggar. It must be delightful to get out into the fresh air especially on a farm.

As you see by my address I am in that 'little village' known as London. I am to be here until the beginning of May when I return to Edinburgh.

My holiday has been most enjoyable. Our term closed at the beginning of April. After that I went to Barrhead with eight or nine students and had a campaign there. We slept in one of the church Halls and looked after some of our meals ourselves, although we always went out for dinner.

It was strenuous but worth while, and I enjoyed every minute. After that I went to Aberdeen for four days Dundee for one and now I am here . . .

With the very best wishes for a glorious holiday. So glad your 'cup is running over'.

> Yours very sincerely
> Eric H. Liddell

'Was it adoration?' Elsa Watson muses. 'I don't really know what it was. I know one thing – it wasn't trying to grab him for oneself. I suppose it was adoration. Yet it was a pretty dignified thing for fourteen-year-olds – no shouting or screaming. It was complete hero-worship. We used to wait, some of us, outside Hope Terrace just to see him coming along.

'Looking back I don't suppose Eric was a wonderful public speaker. But he was so sincere and so electric ... I mean, he shone. It wasn't like just going to listen to a good speaker.'

Years later Elsa was still writing to Eric. She had become a friend of the family, and when his fiancée visited Scotland without him one summer he wrote to Elsa asking her to look after Florence, who was two years younger than Elsa. When Elsa married in 1939, Eric sent her a lithographed picture by a Chinese artist he had saved from death. It was a peony, the flower of China, and he sent it because he liked its beauty and the beauty of the words on it: 'She is the most beautiful in the city (China); her modesty and manner come from God.'

Elsa Watson is quick to leap to his defence when the point is put to her that Liddell was not averse to holding forth on Temperance Society platforms: did that not make him a bit of a kill-joy? A moral tub-thumper? 'Oh, Eric was never that,' she says. 'I don't think he ever went in for tirades against anyone. I think this was one of the reasons he was so effective. He put it in such a humble way, more a matter of suggestion than anything else.'

That was certainly not the opinion of an irate gentleman who wrote to the editor of a Scottish newspaper complaining of Mr Liddell's intolerant language: it is the one and only note of acrimony about Eric Liddell that research has unearthed:

MODERATE DRINKING
A REPLY TO MR ERIC LIDDELL

TO THE EDITOR:

I am one of those who greatly admire Mr Eric Liddell as an athlete and sportsman; but it is with great regret that I observe that he has allied himself with narrow-minded, fanatical teetotallers ... One can have no admiration for the person who advocates compulsory teetotalism for everybody. Having joined the extreme sect of total abstainers, Mr Liddell adopts their intolerant language. Witness his speech at a 'temperance rally' at Glasgow last week. He said – 'Drink took away from character; drink took away from a man all that was honourable.'

These statements are not in accord with fact. Applied to 'drink' *per se* they are untrue; applied to drinking in excess they are true.

There are thousands upon thousands of old athletes in the country – runners, football players, cricketers, golfers and others – who have not been abstainers, but who are living today in good health and prosperity, useful and upright citizens, admired and venerated by their fellow countrymen for their honourable characters.

MODERATE DRINKER of 74 years.

The offending speech had been delivered at the annual temperance rally of the Glasgow Presbytery in the City Hall. The attendance was so great that an overflow meeting had had to be arranged. Liddell was sharing the platform with another leading Scots athlete, Duncan Wright, and a clutch of ministers. He told the audience that two of the greatest problems the Church had to face were gambling and intemperance. Both these evils were sapping the energy of their young people, and the Church had to put up a united front or they would lose ground.

He believed drink had a lot to do with the length of life of the athlete, and the abstainer could add a couple of years to his career. Temptation came to both the athlete and the businessman when they were least able to resist it. Drink took away from the character. Drink took away from a man all that was honourable. Now that, in the context of the times, is actually pretty mild. Even today Liddell's views are not all that far from those of the official bodies who are trying to do something about the social cancer of alcoholism. Although Liddell's language is primarily moral, his implications are social.

Public concern about the problems of pauperism and unemployment, health and hygiene, had continued to grow from its Victorian roots, till in the 1920s it had become a powerful movement. Concern about drunkenness had not abated since Hogarth drew his monitory series 'Gin Lane'. Reformers of every school, social or spiritual, agreed that drunkenness was one of the biggest social problems they had to contend with. If the quality of life was to be improved, they argued, then drunkenness must be suppressed, licences controlled, and the masses educated and restrained.

While a vast army of temperance and abstinence societies marched through this country, the United States was imposing total prohibition of drink on its citizens. The problems of drink were debated *ad infinitum* in the British press, with an impressive barrage of statistical reports on the health risks of alcohol.

Anyone who doubts the seriousness of their convictions just has to look at the famous speech of Lloyd George in 1915 in which he made his views plain enough when a deputation from the Shipbuilders' Federation approached him on the subject. They were worried about the effect of drunkenness on the war effort.

'In dealing with this evil,' Lloyd George replied, 'the feeling is that if we are to settle German militarism, we must first of all settle with the Drink. We are fighting Germany, Austria and Drink, and as far as I can see, the greatest of these deadly foes is Drink.'

Strong stuff. But not as strong as the Rev. James Muir's pamphlet issued by the Church of Scotland in 1930, under the title *The Progress of Temperance in Scotland*. 'Civilization is only possible through temperance,' Mr Muir informed his readers. 'Temperance is faith's strong defence. Intemperance brings downfall and ruin, and the extinction of its light of love ... Alcohol is the foe of the entire man, body, soul and spirit. His bodily functions are all worsened by it. His mind is inflamed, unbalanced and degraded. Conscience is stifled, affections hardened. A fleshly lust that wars against the soul is kindled by it.'

This was doubtless the kind of 'narrow-minded, fanatical teetotaller' to which our 'Moderate Drinker of 74 Years' objected. Eric had probably been influenced by that strain of thought since it was especially prevalent among the missionary community in which he grew up – a belief, it seems, that to touch a drop of alcohol was a sign of moral weakness akin to indulging in an illicit sex binge. The principle was hammered home by some churchmen with a moral condescension which must have infuriated the folk who prided themselves on a temperate intake.

Liddell was too little of a dogmatist for any of that, and certainly too little of a rhetorician. He believed drink was bad for you, and he believed it enough to stand on a platform and tell people so. His speeches are studded with hackneyed epigrams like 'To abstain is safe; to drink leads to crime and poverty.' But, in general, he is coaxing his audience along with the suggestion that abstention has worked pretty well for him, and it might reduce some of the appalling waste in Scottish society if more people tried it.

In the early summer of 1925, Liddell made ready to leave for China. Enormous crowds turned up for the valedictory meetings for him in Edinburgh and Glasgow. The Glasgow occasion required an overflow meeting in a near-by church for nearly 1,000 people who had to be turned away. A few weeks previously the last campaign meeting of the series had packed out the whole of Edinburgh's large Usher Hall, and then a neighbouring church. Hundreds more had been turned away. The Sunday before he left, two church services were held in Liddell's honour, and on the Monday he was astonished to find himself receiving the most amazing send-off any departing missionary can ever have received from Edinburgh's Waverley Station – or from anywhere else.

'That son of yours,' a family friend wrote to Eric's parents on 1 July, 'is so modest I fear he may not think to send you any echo of the many flattering things that happened to him last Sunday and Monday in Auld Reekie.' So the friend, a Mr Bryson, obliges instead. He tells them of the services at Morningside and in Augustine church. 'One of the most striking speeches was that of Professor Russell Scott. It was simply amazing to hear that teacher – not a man to wear his heart on his sleeve – openly acknowledge how he had been sitting at your son's feet, and of his dominant influence in the college. Dr Black said he simply loved your son, and declared he had preached a better sermon than all the ministers in Edinburgh.'

The next day the citizens of Edinburgh were treated to a spectacle as zany as the one they had hurried along to see a year earlier. It was these students again – and that fellow Liddell! A carriage festooned with streamers and ribbons, drawn by a team of students, collected him at the door of the Scottish Congregational College in Hope Terrace and then headed for Waverley Station. Traffic in the city centre stopped as the crowds began to spill on to the street.

Inside the station, Eric was swept along the platform to his train. People were laughing and crying and shouting and . . . yes, someone had started singing. Mr Bryson thinks it was Eric who started up the hymn 'Jesus Shall Reign'. Maybe it was. Whoever did it soon had the entire station belting out hymn after hymn as the train gathered steam and finally pulled out.

'It was such a send-off as no missionary going abroad has ever had in Edinburgh,' Mr Bryson wrote. 'I was glad to be there.'

6

'A Fellow's Life Counts for Far More at This . . .'

When Eric Liddell arrived in Tientsin, his prospective pupils were on strike. Far behind him lay Edinburgh, beautiful genteel Edinburgh with its hills and its castle, its New Town and Old Town, its university and its churches, West End and east-windy, its summer sales and well-appointed tea-rooms. Behind him were the adoring autograph-hunters and a stream of tempting offers of lucrative teaching posts in top-drawer schools. In front of him now lay Tientsin, the capital town of the province of Hopei – large, sprawling, unlovely Tientsin, a divided and confused city in the north-east of a divided, confused and very angry country.

In 1925 Tientsin was already a busy inland port some sixty miles south-east of Peking, lying on the banks of the River Haihe – a river which overflowed its banks nearly every year with often catastrophic results. It had been developing rapidly during the twentieth century and could boast a growing population of about a million people; today it is the largest port in the north, second only to Shanghai among China's industrial and commercial towns with a population that has risen to over four million.

Three main railway lines converged on the city in which Eric was to spend the next twelve years, and it was the terminal for the Trans-Siberian Railway. Seven newspapers hit the streets daily. Electric trams ran over macadamized roads. Miles of wharves teemed with coolies unloading ships from all over the Far East, and crowded suburbs stretched in every direction. It was a city of sharp contrasts. The climate, though not unhealthy with its sea-breezes blowing in from the coast thirty miles away, was one of extremes. Temperatures in the dry, snowless winters often fell below 10°F; in summer they could soar to over 100°F, and there were heavy rainfalls in July and August. When these summer mini-monsoons failed, there were droughts; when they were over-generous, there were equally devastating floods. Occasional violent north winds from Mongolia could bring dust-storms in the spring.

Just as stark were the contrasts in the lives and life-styles of the inhabitants. Mansions rubbed shoulders with hovels; three universities and scores of schools co-existed with widespread illiteracy and age-old superstition. Ex-presidents, retired generals, politicians in retreat, commercial tycoons, leaders of the intelligentsia and sophisticated socialites lived almost next door to sailors and shopkeepers, factory workers and peasants. Almost next door, but not exactly – for Tientsin, 'City of the Celestial Ford', was really two cities, not one.

The first was the old Chinese city with its network of tiny lanes, the equivalent of Edinburgh's Old Town, just to the north-west of the present city centre. It had formerly been surrounded by ancient walls dating back to the early fifteenth century and rebuilt in the nineteenth century, but these had been demolished in the aftermath of the Boxer Rising in 1901. The streets outside the old walls were named after the market-places that used to flourish there – Needle Market Street, Grain Market Street, Donkey Market Street, and so on. In the Devils' Market, antiques and stolen goods were on sale. There was an amusement quarter with theatres, jugglers and acrobats, and the whole place bustled with coolies and shop-keepers, beggars and street-traders, visitors in rickshaws, workers from the salt-pans south of the town, and sailors. There were sailors everywhere.

The large number of sailors frequenting Tientsin gave popularity to the worship of Tian hou ('Celestial Queen'), popularly known as 'The Good Mother'. According to legend, she had been a sailor's daughter who saved her father from shipwreck by remote influence. A magnificent temple was built in her honour just outside the east gate of the Old Town, on the quayside. Sailors flocked there to ask for her protection. In spring, pilgrimages were made to the temple, and each crew would bring a model of their ship. This Temple of the Good Mother no longer exists. There were other temples in and around the Old Town, the Temple of Confucius in particular, and more than a dozen mosques, headed by the Great Mosque to the north-west.

The other Tientsin was the European and Japanese town which grew rapidly round the concessionary areas that had been granted through treaties in the second half of the nineteenth century. These were all south-east of the old 'Chinese town', and lay on either side of the Haihe River. These concessions were, in effect, colonies, run by foreign consuls with their own troops and police forces. Chinese law did not operate inside them. Along the right bank of the river were the British and French concessions, granted in 1858, as well as the Japanese concession (granted after the Sino-Japanese War in 1895), and the German concession of 1896 which came to an end in 1914. On the left bank was the huge Russian concession, along with the Belgian and Italian concessions, and the Austro-Hungarian concession that also ended in 1914. The architecture was and still is a cosmopolitan blend of all the European styles, and a newcomer to this part of Tientsin would find himself travelling the length and breadth of Europe along Victoria Park and the Via Vittorio Emanuele, the Rue du Baron Gros and the Baron Czekam Strasse.

Colourful and cosmopolitan though they may have been, these concessions had mainly been wrested from the Chinese by force of arms, and the foreigners so firmly entrenched in Tientsin were merely tolerated, not liked. Ever since the sixteenth century, China had been a Mecca for European traders, and a magnet for European evangelists – the land of silk and tea, jade and gold, tempting trade-routes and abundant seaports, incense and ancient painted gods. And ever since the Portuguese and Spanish had first arrived in 1514, hungry for wealth and converts, the Chinese had looked upon all Westerners as maurauding pirates, 'foreign devils'.

They had a point. No country was more diligent in seizing the chance of commercial piracy than trade-hungry Britain. Most notorious of all Britain's dealings with China was the opium trade. From the late eighteenth century, British merchants shipped India-grown opium into China in order to pay for Chinese tea and silk, which the Manchu Empire refused to exchange for anything but silver. When the Imperial Government eventually tried to suppress opium-smoking, the British merchants refused to co-operate, and in retaliation some were shut in their factory in Canton in 1839 and had their stocks of opium destroyed. British warships responded, and the Opium War was on. It ended with the Chinese suing for peace in 1842. The Treaty of Nanking legalized the opium trade, opened up Canton and other ports, made the island of Hong Kong a British base, freed British subjects from Chinese law and gave them concession areas to live in. It was the first of what the Chinese called the 'Unequal Treaties'.

Despite the unpopularity of the British, their Protestant missionaries – along with the Dutch and the Americans – did make ground among the sorely oppressed Chinese peasants. There was even a Christian-inspired rebellion, the Taiping Revolution, though this failed to win missionary support and was put down with the help of European military advisers. But if the Taiping Revolution failed, other popular movements were growing. More and more, the Chinese were beginning to protest against exploitation both by their own rulers and by the foreigners flooding the country with factory-made goods which upset the Chinese rural economy, putting thousands out of work and adding to the misery of life under a corrupt and inefficient administration. The Boxer Rising in 1900 was directed against the growing power of Western nations in China and involved attacks on foreigners, foreign imports and Chinese converts to Christianity. This was the frightening upheaval in which Eric Liddell's parents were caught up during the first year of their married life.

The Boxers invaded the legation quarter in Peking and the concessions in Tientsin. Eight countries, including Britain, sent a relief force of 30,000 troops. Their siege and bombardment of Tientsin and Peking broke the back of the Boxer Rising. There was much pillaging and plunder and slaughter. When it was all over in 1901, China had to pay an indemnity of 450 million taels of silver; more foreign concessions were granted, foreign garrisons were allowed to protect the legations, and the Chinese people were burdened with heavier taxes to pay the indemnity. It was then that the walls of old Tientsin were demolished at the insistence of the Europeans because the rebels had been entrenched behind them.

In 1911 a revolution led by the western-educated Dr Sun Yat-sen ended the Manchu Empire and created a Chinese republic, presided over at first by a power-hungry war-lord called Yuan Shi-kai. But it did nothing either to solve the power struggle in China or to alleviate the conditions of the people. Popular movements increased; there were more and more armed uprisings and, after 1915, the number of strikes increased rapidly. Between 1919 and 1921 there were more than 170 strikes involving 250,000 workers.

The real power was by then in the hands of hundreds of warlords who assumed control of whole areas of the country, levying taxes, raising private armies, fighting each other and then negotiating treaties. One war-lord managed to put the last Manchu emperor, who had abdicated in 1912, back on the throne – but only for a week. Another war-lord became dictator of Manchuria with Japanese help. The interminable military campaigns of the war-lords wrecked harvests and caused untold suffering among the people.

As if all that wasn't disruptive enough, China also chose to join the 1914–18 war against Germany (although her one belligerent act was to send coolies to France, where they dug Allied trenches along the Western Front). The real trouble began after the war, when all Chinese hopes of winning some respect for their sovereignty and their territorial integrity were dashed by the Treaty of Versailles of 1919. The Allies allowed Japan to keep all her gains, and they themselves retained all their own pre-war concessions along the Chinese coast. The Chinese got nothing.

Anger and disgust at this betrayal by the Allies fuelled a nationalist demonstration known as the Fourth of May Movement, which in turn sparked off nation-wide strike action. The Chinese Communist Party was born out of these protests in

1920. Among the delegates to the First National Congress of the Communist Party held in Shanghai that year was a young teacher called Mao Tse-tung. In 1922 Chinese strikers tied up all the British ships in Hong Kong, closed factories and paralysed the economy. Strikers near Kowloon were fired on by British troops with many casualties. In June 1925, not long before Eric Liddell arrived in China, 100,000 Chinese went on strike in Hong Kong, and demonstrators were fired on by British and French warships in an incident known as the 'Shakee Massacre'.

By July 1925, the Canton Revolutionary Government was calling itself the National Government, and its army had started to challenge the war-lords in the east. But the revolutionary surge in China was divided into two distinct factions. One was the Kuomintang, the Nationalist Party founded by Sun Yat-sen and now led by Chiang Kai-shek; they favoured a strong national state. The other was the Communists, who wanted a complete transformation of society. These two factions would soon be at each other's throats in another civil war. They would also, before long, be facing invasion from the Japanese, who were already encroaching on Chinese territory in the north-east.

This was the confused, suffering land in which Eric Liddell found himself in the summer of 1925. His father had warned him what to expect.

To those who look on [Mr Liddell had written in his 1924 report from China] it seems that no one party is strong enough to command obedience, and really govern the country. The government of any one party is flouted by some other, although that other may have sworn loyalty to the one in power. It's not surprising that during part of this year Church work has been so difficult . . .

This year we have had the triple evils of war, flood and famine. Any one of these is bad enough, but all three together have made for suffering that is very hard to realize. Ruin has overtaken great numbers of families, and it will never be known how many lives have been lost, through these visitations. Oh, the horror of it all! And to think that so much of it is needless suffering and waste.

And Mr Liddell's latest report had made even gloomier reading:

Words fail to convey to one not conversant with ways Chinese the conditions that exist to make a forecast impossible. The grievances of China have been magnified beyond all recognition. So complex is the situation, so varied are the views expressed, so opposite the conclusions reached, so many the solutions suggested, that one staggers beneath the crushing load. A nation is in travail, seeking to reproduce that which will meet all its aspirations. Whether it will do so or not is another question.

Eric had the reports with him on the long train journey east. The China that he had left Edinburgh for was a powder-keg about to explode.

On its way to Tientsin, the Trans-Siberian Railway passed through a summer resort called Pei-tai-ho. Eric left the train there to join his family, who were taking a holiday by the seaside. Among the welcoming party at the station were some of his future colleagues from the Tientsin Anglo-Chinese College. In some embarrassment they explained to the eager new teacher that the college was currently being boycotted. Some of the students had been intimidated, they told him. The 'May 30th' movement in Shanghai had sent out waves of unrest, which Tientsin was still feeling.

The trouble had started on 14 May, when workers in a Japanese-owned cotton mill in Shanghai went on strike in protest at the dismissal of Chinese workers. The protest was taken up by the students, who demonstrated on 30 May and were fired on by the British police. After this 'May 30th massacre', the Communist Party called on all Shanghai workers, merchants and students to strike. 'Oppose imperialism' was the slogan. The strikes and boycotts fanned out from Shanghai to other centres of foreign concentration like Tientsin, where the Anglo-Chinese College, run by the London Missionary Society, was an obvious target.

The college was the leading British school in North China, a beautiful, grey, towered building on Tientsin's Taku Road. Its 500 pupils were from the middle to upper social class of Chinese families, since the intention from the beginning was that it should cater for the wealthier and more influential element in the population – a group for which missionary societies had made little provision as a rule. The idea was both to offer a top academic training and to teach Christian values to the future leaders of Chinese society. Teaching was in English and organized on an intimate tutorial system, with a staff of five British and twenty-five Chinese masters. Every year the college turned out forty or fifty graduates, who either continued to universities in China or the West, or went straight into the civil service, business or politics.

As well as emphasizing academic achievement and Christian studies, the college was a pioneer of sports in North China. When Dr Lavington Hart had founded the college in 1902, it was unheard of for a student to discard his long, blue cotton gown and go chasing after a ball or an athletic record. It offended every idea of decorum in the tradition. It was the mission schools who pioneered the concept of serious sport and the good old British ideal of sportsmanship and fair play. Liddell said later:

About fifty of the five hundred Chinese pupils are boarders, while, of the staff, four are British and fifteen or twenty are Chinese. On the sporting side the boys play 'soccer', but western games have not yet taken on very much. They are, however, beginning to increase in popularity, and goal posts can be seen on many open spaces.

I do not think that Rugby will ever become a game for the Chinese, for the conditions are too severe . . . the temperature often dropping to 30 degrees of frost. In spite of this, there are British and French Army teams, and a local team of foreigners. Here and there you come across some good 'soccer' players, and there have been Chinese members of Tientsin teams playing against Shanghai and at other places. Although this is the exception rather than the rule, it is an indication that the Chinese are capable of playing our games. *

At the present moment, however, the unsettled state of the country makes it very difficult to stage any programme of sports.

Once they did overcome their distaste, the Chinese idea of sporting endeavour was to play football tripping over their gowns, rush inside at the first drop of rain, refuse to begin the game if they reckoned their side's chances were anything less than a hundred to one, leave the field in high dudgeon with the entire team if a shin was kicked, and dispute vociferously with the referee. Which sounds a lot of fun, but was not to be tolerated by the zealous British. The mission schools saw their championship of sporting play as the highest moral calling. 'It is one of the most productive fields for Christian work,' wrote one of Eric's colleagues, A. P. Cullen, in *Making China's Men*, 'for it remains generally true that the man who is a real sportsman in athletics, who can play the game under all circumstances, fight against odds and disappointments without losing heart or temper, and knows how to take a beating – he is the man who is most likely to be a true sportsman in the greater game of life.'

This was just the job for Eric. But, unfortunately, the students were not even playing the game of lessons right now. The staff had a meeting at Pei-tai-ho and decided to put a bold face on the boycott and try to open the college as usual in September, after the summer break. They all returned to Tientsin to prepare for the new term and Eric joined his family at No. 6 London Mission, their spacious house in the French concession, where, for some reason, the London Missionary Society had based its operations.

The London Missionary Society had been in China since 1807. The LMS Congregationalists were among the first Protestant missions to sail east after the sudden upsurge of British evangelical activity at the end of the eighteenth century. During the next century they were joined by the Baptists, the English Presbyterians, the Anglicans, the Methodists, the Scots Presbyterians, the Quakers, the Plymouth Brethren and, in 1860, the non-denominational China Inland Mission. Jesuits, Dominicans, Franciscans and Augustinians had already been along with the Catholic version.

Before the end of the nineteenth century, the Protestant missions had penetrated every province of China, although they had reached only a small proportion of the whole Chinese population. In the 1920s their activity still remained largely concentrated on the east coast provinces, where four fifths of the 8,000 or so missionaries were working. Most missionary societies refrained from evangelizing on each other's patch, but many Chinese found the profusion of denominations perplexing.

Catholic and Protestant missions, rarely close, were sometimes in bitter competition for congregations.

From early times, the presence of missionaries had aroused antagonism in China – partly derived from their conflict with traditional habits of thought, but more from the growing national sentiment against anything Western. As Evan Luard says in *Britain and China*: 'The missionary was one of the tribulations imposed by Western imperialism. Like railways, extra-territorial rights and foreign control of the Customs, he became a symbol of Chinese humiliation; and those who adopted his faith began to be seen as traitors to the Chinese cause.'

In the late nineteenth century, missions were attacked, missionaries massacred and scurrilous propaganda against them circulated. It culminated in the slaughter inspired by the Boxer Rising. Eric Liddell had been born as the anger of that time was just dying; he returned to China as the the next wave of hostility against the missionaries was beginning to break. An 'Anti-Christian Movement' was initiated by the Chinese, who were angered by the Versailles Treaty and increasingly nationalistic. Missionaries were condemned as disguised imperialists and Chinese Christians as their lackeys. In country areas some were attacked; in the towns, missionary hospitals and schools were subjected to strikes and boycotts.

All this was tough on the missionaries, who had come to China neither to further the aims of their governments nor to support popular rebellions, but to preach about a non-political kind of salvation. The societies had rigid rules about not getting involved in politics, and no missionary felt he had the right to speak out against the policies of his own government or any other, though it may be fair to wonder if some unconsciously used the 'no-politics' rule to escape difficult decisions about the practical implications of the non-materialistic, peace-serving message they were preaching. The missionaries were living, after all, in comfortable houses in the rather cosy, socially self-contained community of a foreign concession, wrested and maintained by force of arms; their potential converts were literally slumming it down the road.

But what could they do? It was a colonial life-style that the missionaries did not invent and could do little to change –

THE FLYING SCOT

Liddell was the hero of the British sporting world in the 1920's. His success as a track sprinter and a rugby three-quarter has never been equalled.

Liddell first came to the public notice when at Edinburgh University in 1920. The Powderhall cinder track was one of Liddell's training haunts, and there among whippets that were training on the same track, coaches told him he had the wrong style for running. Liddell made them eat their words.

In 1921 Liddell received his first rugby cap, when he played for Scotland v. France. In the next four internationals each season Liddell equally featured well and was a regular member of the Scottish team until he decided to concentrate on running as a sport.

The 100 and 220 yards sprints were Liddell's main athletic events and he won both races with monotonous regularity at the Scottish Championships. In 1921, 1922 and 1923 he won both sprints in the Triangular International Contests of Scotland v. England v. Ireland.

In the 1923 Triangular International Contest, Liddell was forced off the track as the runners scrambled for the first corner in the 440 yards. By the time he had regained his feet, he had twenty yards to make up. With great determination he chased the leaders, and at the tape was first over the line where he collapsed.

Following his international success in the 100, the 220 and 440 yards, Liddell toured America, and so great was his reputation that he was besieged by reporters and cameramen from the second he left his ship.

With the approach of the 1924 Olympic Games, Liddell ceased to play rugby and trained for running. When the heats of the 100 metres were announced as being held on a Sunday, Liddell refused to compete because of his religious convictions. No amount of persuasion by team officials could move him, but he decided to run in the 400 metres instead.

LIDDELL REFUSES TO RUN.

In the final of the 400 metres, Liddell drew the outside lane—the least sought after lane, where the runner could not use his opponents who started behind him in a staggered start. At the gun, Liddell leaped from his starting holes and led the field. On he strode, fighting every inch of the way, to victory and the Olympic title.

The city of Edinburgh went wild with joy at Liddell's winning feat. Upon his return, he was pulled in a carriage by cheering crowds through the main streets to be honoured by the civic heads.

In 1925, Liddell went to China to carry out missionary work at the Anglo-Chinese College. His missionary work occupied most of his time and only occasionally did he compete in athletic competitions.

On one of these rare occasions, he was invited to Japan in 1928 to take part in an international sports meeting. Running in his Olympic-winning manner, Liddell outclassed the field in the 400 metres to the delight of the Japanese crowd.

But the crowd did not know was that Liddell's boat back to China was due to leave Japan in only fifteen minutes' time. Liddell mystified officials and spectators alike by continuing to run on round the grandstand and out of the ground.

A waiting taxi rushed Liddell to the docks, but the ship had already cast off from the jetty. Another sprint down the jetty brought Liddell to the edge and, he leaped over the widening gap to land on the after deck.

In 1942, the Chinese province where Liddell carried out his missionary duties, was overrun by the Japanese armies. All the foreign inhabitants were interned in permanent camps. Eric Liddell made the welfare of these prisoners his concern and tended them with such devotion that his own health suffered. In 1945 he collapsed while tending the sick and died in the prison camp.

Cartoon from 'The Victor' (D. C. Thomson and Co. Ltd., Dundee)

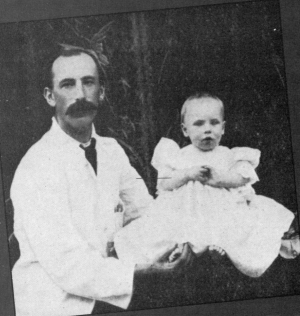

Baby Eric with his father

FAMILY
ALBUM

Eric's wife-to-be Florence when
she was a schoolgirl in China

FAMILY ALBUM

The family. Left to right:
Eric   Jenny   Rob
Mother (Mary)   Father (James)
Ernest

Graduation Day, Edinburgh,
July 1924

Eric Liddell winning the relay race for the British Empire against USA at Stamford Bridge, 19 July 1924

1924 Olympic Games, Liddell winning the 400 metres

Eric's sister Jenny
(now Jenny Somerville)

IN CHINA

Family group, circa 1925

Wedding photograph
of Eric and Florence,
1934, at the Union Church,
Tientsin

A late snapshot of Eric Liddell and Annie Buchan in Northern China

although Eric Liddell reported later that they supported moves for a gradual handing back of the concessions. The missionaries did also take a stand against the opium-smoking with which their greedy governments had cursed the Chinese. It was unfortunate that they had to live in the kind of house Eric now shared with his parents at No. 6 London Mission: big and roomy with a tennis court in front, in a concession guarded by troops and police against any little Chinese annoyances. It made the missionaries all too easy to associate with everything that was most hated in China.

Seen as a clique, as an enclosed social group in their Western compound, the missionaries must have seemed an unattractive lot sometimes. Individually, though, they were loved by the Chinese who knew them. They worked tirelessly; they cared for and loved the people they worked with. When the attacks came, they were often protected by the people they served.

Eric started his first job as a missionary teacher in September. The staff of the Anglo-Chinese College were gratified to see 150 of the 400 students registering that morning, and as many again over the next few weeks. The school was back in business. Eric was there to teach pure science, with chemistry as his special subject, and in his methodical way he began immediately to prepare his lectures and stock up the college laboratory. He was asked to take a few English classes as well, which gave him a good laugh. English had never really been his subject.

He was expected, too, to contribute to the religious life of the college, which he did with gusto. Every morning there was a service of worship, at which one of the British teachers spoke on the day's scripture passage. Eric's old gift of commanding attention with the simplest of talks quickly made him the most popular of the speakers with the boys. Each tutor also held a weekly Bible circle for his class outside school hours. Eric, never one to stand on formality, brought the pupils to his own house.

He did not make remarkable progress as a teacher. He was never at his best standing in front of a class trying to impart organized information. 'I never seemed to get a real grip of the class,' he admitted once with some dejection. It just was not

Eric. The schoolmaster's role was too starchy for him; he adored children and loved being with them, but not in the formal, authoritarian role of the teacher. He always wanted to be laughing with them, helping them to run faster, telling them stories, inspiring them, teasing them, encouraging them, teaching things informally. He worked hard at the role, though, determined as ever to make a go of whatever he put his mind to. His headmaster reported much later that 'as the years have rolled by the momentum has steadily increased'. He had begun to develop the technique.

On the sports field it was a different matter. Eric took over the college athletics and soon had his boys breaking records. He also found time to do a spot of running himself and was soon competing regularly in his long navy-blue shorts against the foreign troops who guarded the concessions. (In an era of long shorts flapping round the knees, Eric's always seemed to look longer than anyone else's!) The first time he ran in Tientsin, spectators who had never seen Liddell in action gaped. It was a relay race, and he streaked away so fast that he picked up thirty yards in the last lap and beat the crack runner of the Fifteenth US Cavalry.

He also lost no time in joining the troops' rugby matches. Rugby in Tientsin was about the most uncomfortable game you could play. The wind came biting down from the Gobi Desert in the north, whipping up the soft, flaky topsoil on their pitch, whisking it into the players' eyes and the cuts on their knees. The players were soon filthy with dust and grime. The former Scottish internationalist revelled in the game, and had soon revived the elusive speed that had been so devastating on the Gracie–Liddell wing. One British soldier was once rash enough to try a lunge as he passed. 'Cor, like a blooming Seagrave,' he was heard to mutter as Eric zoomed away from him.

The athletics track was just as bad as the rugby pitch, and Eric was soon directing the reclamation of a large piece of land for a sports ground. Designs were based on the Stamford Bridge ground in London which had seen some of his most celebrated triumphs, and by the time the work was finished, Tientsin could boast one of the finest running tracks in the whole of the Far

East. Eric himself was one of the first to compete there at the Annual International Athletic Games.

People in Britain had little idea of Liddell's athletic achievements in China. A booklet by the McWhirter brothers called *Get to Your Marks* gives a world ranking for the 400 metres in 1929: 'Liddell, E. – 49·0 secs: date not known – somewhere in China.' But Eric was running well enough in China for the *Peking and Tientsin Times* to express surprise in October 1928 that he had not been invited to join the British Olympic team in Amsterdam that summer.

The irony [wrote the correspondent] is that Liddell would have lent support in one of the weak links, the 400 metres representatives, and his value for the relay races can hardly be over-estimated.

Only a few weeks back, the Scot turned in 21·8 for the 200 metres and 47·8 for the 400. Both these times represent the winning mark at Amsterdam, though neither is quite as good as Liddell's best. His 400 mark, of course, is a world record, and not likely to be beaten for a long time. Liddell's own comment on these two races was 'I think I could do better if I trained for them'.

A man who can improve on 47·8 for the 400 is a marvel. Knowing Liddell as I do, it can be taken for granted that his comment was not a boast, but merely an honest statement of fact. He is a non-smoker and does not drink, but it may be easily understood that however good his normal condition, special training would have given him that extra edge so necessary for Olympic standard. My own opinion is that Liddell is still the best quarter-miler in the world.

Liddell was then not yet twenty-seven years old. The same year he ran in the South Manchurian Railway celebrations for the coronation of the Emperor of Japan. The Japanese and the French Olympic teams were there, their laurels fresh from Amsterdam. 'And it happened, somehow, that I won the 200 and the 400 metres,' Eric told an interviewer a year or two later, underplaying everything as usual.

That interview, conducted while Eric was on furlough in Canada in 1932, is a good example of the ability to deflate pomposity which Eric had practised at primary school and been perfecting ever since. The interviewer, a certain R. E. Knowles, asked in an excessively long-winded way how long he had been a missionary when 'this irregularity' (Liddell's race at the railway celebrations) came to pass.

'Just three years,' said Eric.

'And was there any moaning at the bar?'

'What bar?' murmured Eric.

'The bar of public, religious and clerical opinion. Did the missionary authorities instruct you to moderate your pace?'

'Oh no.'

'Had you had their permission to compete?'

'Oh no.'

'Do you think your pedal prowess is a help to you in your work?' continued the metaphor-struck Mr Knowles indefatigably.

'Sure.'

'Do you ever preach from the text "So run that ye may obtain"?'

'No I'd sooner preach on "The race is not to the swift",' replied Eric, enjoying himself hugely.

Mr Knowles pressed on, and his persistence was rewarded by the nearest anyone ever came to information from Eric about his sporting successes.

'When was your last big race, Mr Liddell?'

'In 1929, I think. I raced the great German runner, Dr Otto Peltzer, holder of the world's 500 metres record, also of the record for the half-mile, also for 1500 metres.'

'And how did you come out?'

'Oh, I won the 400 metres. Peltzer won the 800.'

'And have you ever raced since?'

'Well, now that you speak of it, I believe I did. I believe I won the North China championship in 1930 – but that was all.'

What the relentless Mr Knowles did not manage to elicit from Eric was that, after the race with Peltzer, the German had said to Eric in the pavilion in his broken English:

'You represent Britain at the next Olympic Games?'

'No, I'm too old,' Eric replied.

'How old?'

'Twenty-eight.'

Otto Peltzer roared with laughter. 'Too old? I am thirty-two, and will represent Germany at the next Games in 1932.'

Then, according to the former Royal Scots runner who told the story, Peltzer said, 'You train for 800 metres, and you are the greatest man in the world at that distance.' Peltzer was the world record-holder for the same distance.

Liddell's unorthodox running style turned as many heads in Tientsin as it had in Craiglockart. On one occasion it was more than heads he turned as he flew along the race track and knocked a photographer flying. Head up in the air as usual, he never even saw the poor fellow. Watching from the seats round the arena were his brother Rob and the matron of his hospital from the village of Siaochang, who had wobbled and bumped along the long dirt track on the first motor-cycle ever seen in Siaochang.

Eric was running the 100 metres solo. 'I will never forget Eric coming along with his head back and just tearing along,' the matron, Annie Buchan, recalls. 'A Chinese photographer, not realizing the speed Eric was travelling at, came right into Eric's path with his tripod. Of course Eric came right into him. The photographer went flying, and the tripod too, and Eric fell flat on his face. Rob and I rushed down. Eric was just lying there, and we carried him into a tent unconscious. And when he came round, do you know what he said? "I was just winded," he muttered.'

Another race that has become part of the Liddell legend – so much so that it even featured in a strip cartoon in the British *Victor* comic for boys – was his celebrated 'boat-race' leap. This was the leap that really made the 'Flying Scotsman' nickname stick. Liddell was running at an athletics contest at Darien in 1928. His last race, the 400 metres, was just half an hour before the boat to Manchuria was due to sail. He had to catch that boat. It was twenty minutes from the race-track to the boat, so he ordered a taxi to wait near the finishing tape.

Along thundered Eric, first through the finishing tape. Hardly slackening pace, he made straight for the taxi. Suddenly 'God Save the King' rent the air and he slithered to a halt. Straight as a post he stood there, the taxi a few yards away. 'Go-o-od save the King,' they ended, and he made a lurch for the taxi. But the band struck up the 'Marseillaise' and he had forgotten that the runner who had come in second was a Frenchman. So there he was, stuck like a post again.

'The taxi made it in great time,' he recounted later. 'I took a healthy hop, step and leap, and was on the edge of the wharf before it stopped. The boat was steadily moving out – too far to jump. But a bit of a tidal wave threw it back a little. Then I flung my bags and jumped. I tried to remember in the very act how a gazelle jumps. I felt like one, and I made it; just made it.'

A newspaper correspondent in the car said Eric covered fifteen feet of water. Eric, himself playing it down, said it was less. But legend has credited the Flying Scotsman with a fifteen-foot leap all the same.

The pleasure Eric got out of running – in China as much as in Scotland – the exhilaration and the continued thrill of competition, makes you wonder if he ever regretted the lost opportunity of making sport his life. Did he mind missing the 1928 Olympics? What did he feel when Otto Peltzer told him he could be the world's greatest at 800 metres? Did he not hanker just a little, when he was supervising the chemistry class, or, in later years, tramping the steamy Siaochang countryside with nothing to eat, to be able to devote himself to the sport that was his pleasure?

The redoubtable R. E. Knowles asked him much the same in the Toronto interview. Phrased in Mr Knowles's inimitable style, the question was: 'Are you glad you gave your life to missionary work? Don't you miss the limelight, the rush, the frenzy, the cheers, the rich red wine of victory?'

And Eric's answer was this: 'Oh well, of course it's natural for a chap to think over all that sometimes, but I'm glad I'm at the work I'm engaged in now. A fellow's life counts for far more at this than the other. Not a corruptible crown, but an incorruptible, you know.'

He used to tell his wife he was born lazy and all sports came so easily that he would have been content to make a living from billiards. (He was a dab hand at the billiards table.) 'I think at one time he would very much like to have made sports his career,' she said. 'He did say he would have been quite happy to live by his wits in some kind of sport. But that was before he met D. P. Thomson.'

That meeting at Armadale really had changed his life. He still liked the same things – the lick of the wind on his face as he ran, the joy of breaking the tape at the winning line, the satisfaction of being good at something and knowing it. But he needed more, and once he had made up his mind that it was so, he simply surrendered his life to the God he had accepted. This surrender ought, you feel, to mean weakness. Instead, it is, in Eric Liddell, a form of strength. It was a willing surrender, an unforced obedience; and the mixture of a serene confidence and a genuine humility had a profound effect on those who knew him. They spoke, and still speak of him, in terms that would have made him cringe with embarrassment.

The men who shared a bachelor pad with him after his father's missionary service was over in 1929 and the Liddell family had returned to Scotland without Eric, talked about their months in the Tientsin flat as 'the richest of their lives'. One of them, George Dorling, the surgeon, said simply: 'We three were miles below the standard Eric set for himself. But he was always our friend. I knew that every time I could count on Eric. Nothing ever shocked him. His love was too great to be shocked.'

Another flatmate, Scotsman David McGavin, described him as 'a perfect Christian gentleman'. The eulogies are endless.

'I never heard Eric say an unkind word of anyone,' said another.

'Eric was the most Christ-like man I knew.'

'Eric had a great sense of humour, but if work had to be done, that came first.'

Someone once spotted a fly on a biscuit when they were being entertained to coffee and, mindful of the danger of germs, warned Eric not to touch it. 'But this was the biscuit that Eric was careful to take,' says the story-teller. 'His action was not intended as a rebuke to me – that would never occur to him – but to make certain that no one else should suffer discomfort as a result of eating a biscuit defiled by the fly.'

Of course, these were the tributes of men to whom words like 'Christ-like' and 'Christian gentleman' were everyday language, and whose own lives were dedicated to the attainment of the kind of qualities they saw in Eric Liddell. They spoke in a more fulsome way than we are used to today, and it is always tempting to sanctify a good man when he is dead. All the same, they point to a most remarkable character.

He seemed to get his strength and self-discipline and his air of quiet serenity from his early-morning sessions of prayer, meditation and Bible study. He would come out from that and stride through the rest of the day as though the Sermon on the Mount was still ringing in his ears. Whatever it was that he received in those morning sessions he spent the rest of the day giving out to others. He measured his standards by it, and if he thought those standards had slipped, he was as stern with himself as he declined to be with others. Somewhere in this daily discipline of faith lay the secret of the man, perhaps the secret of how he ran.

David McGavin once asked him if he ever prayed that he would win a race. He replied, 'No, I have never prayed that I would win a race. I have, of course, prayed about the athletic meetings, asking that in this, too, God might be glorified.'

The young girl he was about to start courting said, years later: 'He believed in praying. One hour every morning it was. I tried to keep up with him but, boy, I was away behind him. I think that was the secret of his life. He would think through the whole day and what he had to do, and that was where he would get the strength to do it.'

He was never too busy to see the Chinese students who called on him, day or night; he was never too pious to lark about with the youngsters – 'He had a touch of devilry in him,' said one later – and usually led the way in any mischief. 'How could you behave like that when you were with Mr Liddell?' scandalized mothers would scold, little dreaming that Mr Liddell had been in the thick of the mischief himself. His sense of humour defused many a conflict among the missionaries. In the missionary compound, tensions and quarrels were as rife as they always are when strong-minded people are living close together. 'Oh, the missionaries were very stuffed-shirts,' said the son of a missionary who was then at Tientsin Grammar School with Eric's brother, Ernest, and future sweetheart, Florence. 'Especially the evangelicals. They felt they were God's chosen people and the others were letting them down all the time and dropping moral standards. Eric wasn't like that. He could live on both sides.'

But he would let no one walk over him. There was a determined streak in Eric never far from the surface, whether he was refusing to run on a Sunday – or choosing a bride . . .

7

'I Didn't Even Know
He Was Courting'

When Eric Liddell told his friends in July 1930 that he was
engaged to be married, they were flabbergasted.

'I didn't even know he was courting,' said his close friend, Bob
Knight, whose ship was in the harbour at Tientsin at the time.

Even the girl in question had not been aware that Eric was
assiduously courting her. She was only seventeen years old at
the time, ten years younger than Eric. Her name was Florence
McKenzie, the daughter of Canadian missionaries whom Eric
had known for years. She had been in Eric's brother Ernest's
class at school, she played the piano in the Union Church Sunday
school, where Eric was superintendent and where she had once
been a pupil.

'I was terribly naive,' she explains. 'Eric had become such a
part of the family that I just didn't notice anything. Of course I
was desperately in love with him, but I just couldn't get over the
fact that he wanted to marry me.'

But tea-drinkers in a popular Tientsin café called Kiesslings
had begun to suspect; and friends of Florence had guessed weeks
before. Eric had always taken an interest in young people, but
this was ridiculous. He was showing a remarkable enthusiasm
for taking whole gangs of them on picnics, for walks, or for tea
at Kiesslings. The trouble was, a chap could not just ask a girl to
go out with him (according to the rules of the society in which

they lived), especially if she was just out of school and only seventeen. Subtlety was called for. So Eric, observing the conventions with his usual aplomb – and sending them up ever so slightly – simply invited Florence's whole circle of friends and classmates whenever he wanted to take Florence out. Tennis parties at the Pei-tai-ho beach resort helped, too, and the McKenzies were getting used to the sight of Eric at their front door, breezily suggesting that the entire family come for a walk in the summer rain.

Florence was planning to go to Canada to train as a nurse, but she failed her French exam and – 'Oh, I was just in a terrible state about it. I thought I wouldn't be allowed into the hospital without my senior matric exam, so I was talking about giving up the whole idea.'

That was when Eric spoke up. Not for one minute must she think of giving up, he said. And, by the way, did she fancy coming out for a bit of a walk, because there was something he wanted to ask her?

'I accepted him right away,' says Florence, who now lives in Canada. Her mass of black, curly hair is grey now, but she still has the bubbling vivacity and rich Canadian accent that Eric knew. She was a bright, happy girl, with the same uncomplicated approach to life as Eric. Quiet but sunny-natured, she had a down-to-earth quality and strength of mind that show at once in her conversation. This was not the kind of woman to have had much time for excessive piety.

'I can't *stand* these people who are so goody-goody and holy-holy,' she says. 'They bring out the worst in me and make me want to go the opposite way. Eric wasn't like that. His wonderful sense of humour saved him from ever being like that. He had a poker-faced humour, and you had to watch his eyes very carefully. They usually gave him away, if you looked closely.'

People often mention those give-away eyes of Eric Liddell's. Teachers when he was at school soon learned that the only way to catch him out was to read his eyes. And he needed some catching-out as a youngster. His chief characteristic, which remained the main weapon in the Liddell armoury, was a look of such cherubic innocence that he was usually the last to be suspected of any schoolboy pranks he instigated.

'Liddell,' the headmaster told him once in class, in a sudden burst of enlightenment, 'I am beginning to think you are not as good as you look.' And he wasn't. But he had a smile that seldom failed to get him out of trouble. This instinctive ability to disarm opposition always served Eric well. He got his own way with such quiet charm that people hardly noticed they were giving way – and that went for the Japanese invaders in China as much as for the members of his own family. He scandalized his mother once by walking the streets of douce Edinburgh in a lurid shirt he had bought in Hawaii. 'Eric, you can't go out in that!' she wailed; but Eric, who loved wild colours and didn't care what the neighbours thought of his shirt, just grinned and wore it. 'He knew what he wanted,' says Florence. 'He was very sweet with his mother, but he just went his own way.'

When Florence accepted his proposal that day in Tientsin, Eric immediately sent home for a diamond ring. He wanted one with five diamonds in a row, the same as his mother's. So his mother and sister went to a jeweller's in Edinburgh and bought a ring, which they sent to China. As soon as it arrived, he and Florence became officially engaged. It was to be a long engagement, like his parents' had been. Florence left soon afterwards to do her nurse's training in Canada, and it was four years before they married in Tientsin in 1934.

Meanwhile Eric went home on his first furlough to Scotland. After a stay in Toronto with his fiancée and her family, he arrived back in Edinburgh, where his parents were now living (his father had retired from the mission field in 1929), in the summer of 1931.

It was seven years since he had won his gold medal at the Paris Olympics, six years since his *annus mirabilis* of evangelistic speaking up and down the country. But Scotland had not forgotten him. He was immediately swooped on by the sporting world, the religious world, the temperance world – and the newspapers. His welcome back was tumultuous. For thousands of people in Scotland, the Olympic champion who had turned missionary was still a national hero.

His formal purpose in returning to Scotland was to take a course of studies at the Scottish Congregational College in Edinburgh with a view to being ordained; but so great was the demand to see and hear him speak that a college committee had to be set up to co-ordinate his schedule. He spoke wherever he was called: at sporting rallies all over Scotland, and from pulpits in churches of all denominations, not just in Scotland but in England and Northern Ireland as well. At a great 'Public Welcome Home Meeting' in Edinburgh, attended by leading churchmen and sporting luminaries like G. P. S. Macpherson, the Scottish rugby captain, Eric Liddell set the uncompromising tone of all the speeches that were to follow:

'We are all missionaries. We carry our religion with us, or we allow our religion to carry us. Wherever we go, we either bring people nearer to Christ, or we repel them from Christ. We are working for the great Kingdom of God – the time when all people will turn to Christ as their Leader – and will not be afraid to own him as such.'

Apart from the evangelism, he could not avoid talking about the current political situation in China, about which so much had been written in the press in the preceding months. To meeting after meeting he tried to explain the growth of patriotic nationalism in China and the Chinese hostility towards foreigners, even towards the missionaries who were working there in a spirit of selflessness.

He took his message about Chinese nationalism to a short series of packed meetings in Belfast – a brave thing to do in the political climate of Northern Ireland at the time.

'In a city such as Tientsin there are colleges in what are termed the concessions – areas taken over by foreign powers. Chinese public opinion, strengthened by a growing national feeling that other nations had taken from her what should be hers, has been asking that these concessions should be given back.

'I don't want to go into the political aspect of the question, not being a politician myself. But just glancing at the matter I feel it would be extremely difficult to give this land back immediately; but our policy – and the people in Tientsin are trying to do it – is gradually to hand it over. I think that this method will not only cause less complication between nation and nation, but is the most Christ-like way in which it can be done.'

One large rally in Edinburgh that must have pleased him as much as any was held by the Lord's Day Observance Society of

Scotland. Here, Eric Liddell moved a resolution that was seconded by a young minister, a future Moderator of the General Assembly of the Church of Scotland called Leonard Small, then newly ordained to St John's Church, Bathgate. The resolution, which was carried unanimously, declared:

That the meeting is of the opinion that the increasing use of the Lord's Day for games and recreations, however harmless in themselves, is detrimental to the highest interest of the youth of the country, as well as adding to the amount of unnecessary labour of other people; and calls on all young people's organizations to give full consideration to this aspect of the question.

Eric Liddell's unbreakable stand on the principle of Sunday observance at the Paris Olympics had been no flash in the pan. He was to stand by it all his life, even in the Japanese internment camp in China where he was to pass his last months, and where he was responsible for all sporting and recreational activities. There was only one occasion on which he broke the Sabbath there – but that story comes later.

In June 1932, Eric Liddell was ordained to the ministry in the chapel of the Scottish Congregational Church. His furlough was now over, and it was as the Rev. Eric Liddell that he set off for China. He travelled by way of Canada, so that he could visit his fiancée in Toronto. Florence was then in the middle of her training course at the Toronto General Hospital. In Toronto he also met the British Olympics athletics team, who had stopped off for some training on their way to the 1932 Olympics at Los Angeles.

It was there that he also met that egregious newspaperman, Mr R. E. Knowles. The tone and prominent display of the interview he published shows something of the extent of Liddell's world fame at that time. The article concluded with a coy aside from Mr Knowles to all the Canadian women who must be simply *dying* to know why Eric was lingering in Toronto – hardly the most direct route from Britain to China. For these women, he wrote, 'who would not smile again for a week if I stopped right here, I have been permitted to say that a certain missionary-ess, a nurse in training at Toronto General Hospital . . . is the occasion of Mr Eric Liddell's divine detour'.

And with a last arch aside: 'And, as I bade my now dear friend goodbye, I advised him, should church officials query his wanderings, to plead that the added mileage is due to reasons of health – that he was suffering from a rush of Toronto to the head.'

Eric escaped back to Tientsin, where he was due to resume work at the Anglo-Chinese College at the start of September. He now had extra responsibilities; in addition to being superintendent of the Union Church Sunday school, he took over as secretary of the college and chairman of the Games Committee, and was put in charge of the religious activities of the college. Life at the college was changing; there had been no more strikes, but since Dr Lavington Hart retired in 1930, there had been a succession of Chinese principals, and relations were sometimes uneasy.

Outside the college with its daily round of teaching and studying, and its beach parties at Pei-tai-ho, a vicious civil war was being waged between the Communist Red Army and the Nationalists under Chiang Kai-shek for the control of China's political soul. There were massacres, burnings and lootings all over the country. In 1931, Japan invaded Manchuria in northeastern China on a trumped-up pretext; in the following year, the Japanese launched a savage assault on Shanghai, then as now the largest and busiest port in the Far East. Despite the gallant defence put up by Chiang Kai-shek's Nineteenth Route Army, large parts of Shanghai were flattened by carrier-bombers and naval gunfire before Britain stepped in to arrange a ceasefire.

Tientsin itself was unaffected by the strife to north and south of it, and the college carried on as usual. The only recorded reaction from Eric Liddell is in a letter he wrote after one of his classes was ordered by the government to take up military drill: 'Although I hate war, and feel the attitude of Christian people to it is going to be one of the greatest challenges in the future, yet it *has* smartened up some of the lads quite a bit.'

During this period Eric was preoccupied with his personal affairs. His father, who had been such an inspiration to him

111

always, died in the autumn of 1933, and Eric wrote a stream of comforting, affectionate letters to his bereaved mother:

When this letter reaches you near the end of February the first flowers of spring should be starting up. Surely by then the snowdrops should be out, and a little later will come the crocuses and daffodils. Jenny's garden will soon begin to bloom again. You must go out there, Mother, and stay with her, especially at that time of year. I am glad that I have recently had a furlough and been with you, for now I can picture it all so clearly and seem to know what you are doing.

At the same time he was having his house in Tientsin redecorated for his wedding, which was planned for the spring of the following year, 1934. Florence passed all her nursing exams in Toronto that winter, and left for China at the beginning of February. Five weeks later she was at Tientsin, and on 27 March 1934 they were married in the Union Church there. The front-page report in the *Tientsin and Peking Times and North China News* is splendidly flowery, equal to the British press reports of any 1930s society wedding in London or Edinburgh:

There was a large attendance of foreigners and Chinese at the Union Church this afternoon when the Rev. Eric H. Liddell, the well-known Olympic champion, was united in matrimony with Miss Florence Jean McKenzie, the daughter of Mr and Mrs Hugh McKenzie, well known and much respected residents of Tientsin. Prior to this the civil ceremony took place this morning at HBM Consulate before M. S. G. Beare, HBM Consul.

The nuptial knot was tied by Rev. Eric Richards (Minister of Union Church) assisted by Dr Murdoch McKenzie, who, besides having been a resident in China for the past forty-three years, also christened the bride. To the strains of *Lohengrin's Wedding March* the bride entered on the arm of her father who gave her away.

The bride's wedding dress, which was also her mother's wedding dress, was of white satin with lace veil trimmed with a sprig of orange blossoms, and she carried a bouquet of pink carnations. The lace veil had also been worn by Miss Liddell, the sister of the bridegroom, at her own wedding. The bride was attended by Miss Gwyneth Rees as bridesmaid, who was charmingly gowned in green silk lace with green hat to match and she carried a bouquet of pink carnations.

The best man was Dr George Dorling, and the ushers Mr Gerald

Luxon, Mr R. Schmuser, and Mr E. S. Box. Mrs Hugh McKenzie, the bride's mother, wore a black georgette dress, trimmed with lace, with black hat to match, and she carried a bouquet of pink carnations. The church was artistically decorated for the occasion with flowers and plants by Mrs Gerald Luxon and Mrs C. H. B. Longman. Mr C. W. W. Lewis officiated at the organ.

After the religious ceremony a reception was held at the home of the bride's parents, No. 70 Cambridge Road, and was attended by a large number of the many friends of the happy couple. The guests were received under a large silver bell covered with ferns and pink carnations. Dr Murdoch McKenzie proposed the health of the bride and bridegroom, which was suitably responded to by the bride. [It was, in fact, Eric who replied to the toast.]

Eric, who, like most missionaries' children, had spent much of his childhood and youth separated from his parents, slipped easily and happily into family life. Two daughters came along in quick succession, first Patricia, and then Heather. When Heather was born there was the usual family debate over a name for the baby. Eric offered to solve the problem by putting two pieces of paper in a hat, one with her final choice, one with his. With great solemnity he drew out a paper with the name 'Heather' on it – his own choice. It was only later that he confessed he had written 'Heather' on both bits of paper. It says much for Florence's sense of humour that she accepted the decision, and much for the quality of their marriage. They laughed a lot and shared everything.

Eric Liddell turned out to be the typical proud father. *His* children were, quite simply, the most perfect creatures that had ever been born on this earth. He adored them. His letters home to Scotland were full of momentous details like the first teeth, the first steps, the first falls, the sleeping averages. It's interesting to note his athlete's way of describing baby Patricia's progress in walking: not 'She took so-and-so many steps today', or 'She made it right across the room', but – 'She did twelve yards on her own'.

Their family life was a very happy one, considering the circumstances they were in. They used to go on bicycle-rides all together, Patricia on a small seat on the cross-bar of father's bike, Heather in the basket at Florence's handlebars. Of that beautifully happy marriage, which was to last only eleven years, Florence was to write to D. P. Thomson:

I will always thank God that I had the rare privilege of being Eric's wife. I think we had more fun and happiness in our eleven years together than lots of couples have in a whole lifetime of married life. He was a perfectly grand husband and so sweet with the children. Patricia, the eldest, has vivid memories of him, but unfortunately Heather's memories aren't quite so vivid, because ever since she was ten months old, Eric was never with us more than six weeks at one stretch.

Not only did Eric Liddell see little of his second daughter, Heather; he never saw his third daughter, Maureen, at all, for the time was coming when he would have to leave his family for very long periods – and eventually for ever.

The first stirrings that were to lead to these enforced separations came barely a year after his marriage, in the spring of 1935. There was a shortage of missionaries in the countryside, and the Tientsin Anglo-Chinese College was thought by some to be getting an unfairly large share of the available London Missionary Society staff. Eric was asked by the District Council if he would agree to go and help with the work at Siaochang, where the Liddells had been born and raised and where his older brother, Rob, was already working as a missionary doctor. It was a dismaying prospect for a newly married couple with an infant daughter. Siaochang was in an area devastated by war and drought. It was desperately in need of help, but, on the other hand, moving from Tientsin would mean breaking up the family, for Eric would have to be away for months on end. It would also mean leaving classes of intelligent young students to work among illiterate peasants and, of course, the end of the cosy tennis parties, the teas at Kiesslings. Besides, Eric's Chinese wasn't fluent enough yet, and he would have considerable difficulty in communicating with the unlettered souls in his care.

It was an appallingly difficult choice for a young couple to have to face, and at first they decided that the move would not be a good idea. In his annual report to headquarters in London, Eric wrote:

The summer brought me face to face with the question as to whether I felt called to country work, seeing that that section of the work was so understaffed. I thought over it then, and have been thinking over it ever since, and cannot but feel that I am more equipped for educational work, both by training and temperament. Besides, at the present time it would make it extremely difficult in the college to reduce numbers.

But gradually the pressure began to build up – economic pressure on the London Missionary Society, and the private pressure of Eric's own conscience. In 1936 the District Council decided that Eric should be released from the college for four months to explore 'country work' at first hand. By the beginning of 1937, his mind was made up. He would go.

Eric Liddell was no martyr to asceticism: he liked the good things of life and had an easy-going nature, with no particular relish for changes or difficulties for their own sake. Life was going just fine, thank you: an adored young wife, two adored young daughters. His colleagues at the college urged him to stay on at Tientsin, saying that he was badly needed there, and Eric tried hard to believe them. But, in the end, he decided, after much prayer, that it was his duty to go.

Florence Liddell was later to write to D. P. Thomson:

It was a big step, involving many changes, and it took him a long time to be sure he was doing the right thing. There were friends on both sides of the question who felt very strongly about it. However, after much prayerful consideration of all the points involved, he felt God was calling him to the country, and I think it was quite obvious he did the right thing. He loved the work, his health improved, and I think he blossomed out in a new way.

A missionary community, once convinced that one of their numbers is on the wrong track, can be a formidable force to be reckoned with. Eric Liddell was made to feel all the weight of their disapproval, their condemnation, their anger at what they considered his foolhardiness in throwing away all his vital educational work in the big city. 'It really hurt him,' said Florence, 'but he never let on. That was one place where I learned that he could take criticism.'

But nothing would shake Eric's resolve once he had decided

what was the right course to take: in December 1937 he left to join his brother Rob in Siaochang. The wheel was coming full circle.

8

'It Is Wonderful To Feel at One with the People'

Imagine Siaochang in the 1930s. It is a village in the heart of the Great North Plain in southern Hopei. The fields lie ruined by drought, locusts and the depredations of marauding soldiers. Big families are squashed into tiny houses; hunger or disease is in nearly every home. These are simple people who cannot read, but who love to learn. They are frightened people who know that their next meal, even their lives perhaps, may depend on which Japanese soldier, or Chinese guerrilla, or wandering bandit may pass through next. They are slow-moving, farming people who are having it hard.

Here was a China unchanged by the centuries. There were still girls whose feet were bound, crushed and maimed from the age of five, with the toes tucked under the sole. The damp cotton bandages were changed every day, the feet massaged and bound again, to make these feet grow unnaturally small. No respectable man wanted to marry a girl unless her feet were bound. With unbound feet, she would rank as a slave girl. But, in the countryside around Siaochang, every peasant was a slave – to feudal lords, to war, to hunger, drought and disease. Faithfully they appealed to their many gods. One was the kitchen god, with its image pasted on the wall. Every New Year the picture of the kitchen god was changed for a new one; the old picture was then burned, but only after the god's mouth had been smeared with sugar, to make sure that it could only say sweet words when it reported the family's behaviour to the authorities in heaven.

On the night of 7 July 1937, a few months before Eric Liddell's arrival at Siaochang Mission, Japan had launched a full-scale invasion of China following a minor military incident at the Marco Polo Bridge west of Peking. The Japanese had been encroaching on Chinese territory for years, greatly helped by Chiang Kai-shek's obsession with fighting his Communist rivals. In his preoccupation he ignored not only the invader but the appalling plight of the peasantry in North China, whose livelihood was withering in droughts, or being washed away in the floods that afflicted the north in the 1930s.

Encouraged by the submissive attitude of the preoccupied Nationalists, the Japanese penetration of North China continued, heading for Chungking on the Yangtse River. Eventually, in August 1937, the Nationalists and the Communists joined forces in an anti-Japanese United Front – a reluctant and short-lived co-operation. The main body of the Red Army stationed in the north-west was reorganized into the Eighth Route Army of the National Revolutionary Army, and an extensive guerrilla campaign against the Japanese-held railways swung into action. The people of the Siaochang district were to learn all about the Eighth Route Army in the days to come, as the fortunes of battle swayed this way and that.

The Japanese campaign against the Chinese was fierce, and designed to humiliate. They adopted blitzkrieg bombing and terror tactics to encourage quick surrender. By the end of 1939 – the year in which the Second World War started for the Western world – Japan would control the main lines of communication and the major cities of eastern China, such as Shanghai and Tientsin and Peking itself. But they failed to dominate the rural areas, and at about the time when Eric Liddell moved into the country, Chinese guerrilla units were beginning to operate behind enemy lines. Whenever they attacked a blockhouse, or blew up an ammunition train, the Japanese took immediate reprisals against the civilian population.

The people of Siaochang were right in the middle of these

assaults and counter-assaults. The two main railway routes, from Tientsin to Shanghai, and from Peking to Hankow, passed within forty miles to the east and fifty miles to the west of Siaochang. The railway lines were in the hands of the Japanese, but the land in between was controlled by the Chinese. The fighting was interminable, and the people in the district looked to the missionaries for protection. The mission compound at Siaochang had a hospital, which was always crowded out, and a church with refuge for 500, where the women and children hid during attacks. There was also a big girls' school, for it was only the missions that undertook to educate girls in China at that time.

The church, the school and the living quarters were inside the mud wall which surrounded the compound. Over the front gate a sign read: 'Chung, Wai, I Chai' – 'Chinese and Foreigners, All One Home'. The Chinese had put up the sign when the buildings had had to be rebuilt after destruction in the Boxer Rising – that earlier conflagration which had sent Eric's parents fleeing from their first mission post in China.

Siaochang was the centre of a wide field of activity covered by the London Missionary Society on the Great Plain. It was a district the size of Wales, and Eric was expected to cover it as an itinerant evangelist, visiting churches, advising the Chinese preachers, sharing the lives of the people he visited, answering their questions, dealing with their problems. He needed all his celebrated patience for the job. The dreary treks on foot or by bicycle across the miles of either parched or flooded land were enough to sap the strength and weary the spirit without having to dodge bandits and guerrillas, and explain your business and your destination to a succession of Japanese gun-barrels. Outdoor preaching meant soakings or scorchings, depending on the season. When he stayed in villages, he went hungry if his host did, and slept on the floor and shared the misery of those who shared their roof with him. Sometimes he found villages burned out, the menfolk shot dead, their families numb with grief.

The sufferings of this area had started years before the Japanese moved in, when the civil war was raging and anti-Christian feeling was at its height. While Eric was teaching chemistry in Tientsin, the missionaries of Siaochang had been in the thick of the strife that was convulsing the land. Miss Annie Buchan, now a sprightly octogenarian living in Peterhead in the north-east of Scotland, but then the Scottish matron of the hospital, recalled later, in a booklet called *Adventure in Faith*, the perils of 1927 that were being repeated in 1937.

In the spring of 1927 we had a message from the British Consul ordering us to evacuate for Tientsin without delay. We had no choice. After consulting our Chinese colleagues we set off with a heavy heart; but, fortunately, after an absence of five months we were allowed to return . . .

There came another order to evacuate in May 1928. Anti-foreign feeling had been stirred up, and we were in a country station a long way from the railway. It was considered advisable for us to get out while it was still possible. This time, however, we were rebellious. We wanted to take the risk, but the Chinese warned that the uprising was serious. They advised us to go. Saying goodbye was unforgettable. One well-meaning friend said, 'You are fortunate. The British Consul will take care of you. We have no one to protect us, we have to depend on God.' It is not difficult to imagine how we felt leaving our dear friends in this way, to face whatever was to come.

Unforgettable also was the five-day journey travelling zig-zag across the Plain, avoiding known routes in fear of meeting soldiers, or being caught between the opposing armies. There were also renegade soldiers on the rampage, plundering for money in order to help them escape from either army. Our transport was the usual mission springless cart, with the Rev. W. F. Rowlands in charge of us women – Mrs C. Busby stayed behind: someone had to stay, as the compound was full of refugees.

We had not gone far when our carter took fright and refused to go any farther. Suddenly, soldiers seemed to be springing from nowhere, demanding our mules. One soldier covered us with his gun while another unharnessed the mules. After pleading, and finally giving some money, they left us with one mule, the least able to carry our load. Our carter saw that it was as dangerous at that stage to return as to move forward, so we moved on. But, where could we stay the night? Soldiers were on the march all around us. Each village we came to seemed lifeless. Not a soul to be seen. Not a sound except, now and then, the cry or whimper of a baby.

To our delight, at one village we saw the sign of a Methodist Mission. When we knocked, a man opened the door, just a slit, and whispered that everyone had left. He was obviously scared to let us in but, being desperate, we pushed our way inside. To our surprise there were more Chinese within hiding from the soldiers. One man had been a patient in our hospital and knew Mr Rowlands who had baptized him five years earlier. His name was Mr Han, and he did everything for our comfort as far as possible within a stripped building. We ourselves were safely indoors, but what about our cart? The mule was brought in, and the cart dismantled and brought under roof, for fear of the soldiers!

It had been blowing a dust storm, and we were very grimy, and very tired. Pastor Han and Pastor Hu pleaded with us to stay and hide with them; but, as in many a tight corner, we prayed for guidance and felt assured that we should press on regardless of danger. We lay down as we were, in our clothes, ready to start at daylight.

Being already dressed, and there being no water to wash, we did not delay. A cup of tea was brought to us and, after the cart had been made ready, we were off. The weather was unusual. We had been through a dust storm, and now it was heavy, blinding rain with head wind. The carter was not in a good mood. He turned, and saw me shivering, my teeth chattering with the cold. 'God isn't favouring you now,' he said. But the bad weather was in our favour and we were not molested, although we had not gone far when we met a band of soldiers. They spoke to us, and when they knew we had come from the Jesus Mission at Siaochang they were friendly and sang hymns. Other soldiers passed us in a hurry to go on.

We had been told of how soldiers plundered the poor village people, and now we were seeing them at work – kicking open doors, pushing their swords through them, and heard the cries of the terrified people inside. There was, of course, nothing to plunder from us, but once again we felt ashamed to go free. The band of soldiers were also ashamed for us to see what their fellow soldiers were doing and offered to escort us. We did not want that, however, knowing that we would be safer on our own.

Very soon another band of soldiers caught up on us. They blamed us for having a bodyguard and for breaking Treaty Rights. Finally, they all came along with us, making us walk while they took it in turn to ride upon the cart. Things were looking ugly. We were willing to walk but were not happy about the uneasy peace. Fortunately for us, the enemy was on their tail and they ran off in front as fast as they could.

For the missionaries of Siaochang, life seemed to be a

succession of alarms and excursions. The civil war continued to disrupt their work, even before the Japanese moved in.

One day a general of one of the Chinese armies arrived with his soldiers, a man of both wealth and power, and a number of wives and concubines. I escorted him round the hospital and his eyes filled with tears at the sight of so many babies ill and starving. Because of the civil war, I explained, we could not get milk, which could be more nourishing than the local bean curd milk. Nothing was said, but, a few days later, a number of cases of tinned milk arrived, a gift from the general, a man who had no use for religion and was hardened at the sight of blood on the battlefield. What could have happened to have stirred and softened his heart, at the sight of babies starving from lack of nourishment? I don't know, but he never had another opportunity of doing a good deed for, shortly afterwards, his army was defeated and he himself murdered about a mile from Siaochang.

Eric's brother Rob and his wife and daughter joined the hospital staff around this time. Rob had trained at Edinburgh University as a doctor and good doctors were worth their weight in gold at Siaochang, where the mission hospital had over a hundred beds and was expanding all the time. Although the hospital had a well-established baby clinic, the rate of infant mortality was astounding. A frightening number of babies died from convulsions in the first few weeks of life, mainly through tetanus. The most common method of post-natal care of the new-born infant was to fill a piece of rag with earth from the ground and wrap it round the umbilical cord: the baby was then laid aside unwashed.

The Chinese had no cows' milk, and rice water was not sufficient for baby feeding; also, the mothers, who spent a lot of time working in the fields, seldom had sufficient milk. To offset this deficiency the mission hospital started a soya-bean milk kitchen, where beans were crushed and prepared with the necessary addition of calcium and sugar. It was cheap for the Chinese to buy, and tinned milk was unobtainable. Midwifery was still hazardous – and full of surprises. Annie Buchan admitted a woman who was ill with a supposed abdominal tumour and was taken into the operating theatre for examination:

'she promptly gave birth to four baby boys, one after the other. Sadly, all had been dead for some time.'

Eric had spent the first five years of his life in Siaochang with his parents and many of the people there remembered them. His father's winning personality had left its mark and ensured Eric a welcome in many a village. He went round at first with an interpreter called Wang Feng Chou, and their day would start with a wobbly bicycle ride. Eric described it once in a vivid dispatch:

It was a perfect day with not a cloud in the sky and a slight north wind blowing us along. Wang is not a good rider, so we went along slowly. He knew all the short cuts, and it's very much easier when you needn't worry about the road. We stopped at a small place, just near Chuan Tyu. It was a carpenter's shop, but also an inn. We only waited about ten minutes, and during that time told the old man what we were doing. The shop was busy: they were preparing many poorer coffins than usual. The old man – about eighty – had the fine courtesy of old China. We left him and passed by the edge of a temple with a large straight tamarisk tree – quite a landmark. In the distance we could see the Japanese flag waving over the town of Chuan Tyu. Periodically their forces, which are very small, go out on their expeditions, but that day we met no one.

The people in the village were busy spinning thread, and as the making of native cloth this year brings in so much the people are all busy at it. The crops in Nan Kung have been largely a failure, only three or four tenths of the usual, and so the making of cloth is helping people to find a living.

As the sun was setting we reached Wang Feng Chou's village and he found me a place to stay. I stayed in the home of the father of one of the Siaochang School boys. It was a very large family of some twenty odd. Last year cholera carried away four of the family within a very short time.

The boy in Siaochang is in his last year at school. His wife turned out of her room to let me have it. They looked after me very well indeed and were kindness itself. They met each night in my room, and the people from round about gathered with us. We started with hymns which I slowly taught them and by the end of the week they had learned several new ones. The old women are the problem, they learn so slowly compared with the others. Each day, I went out to nearby places and had meetings in the mornings and the afternoons, leaving about 4 p.m. so as to be back before the sun set.

The whole of this area is riddled with the Eighth Route Army troops. Schools are opened and all below forty-five are forced to go to them. As you come to these villages, the person on guard often has a slate with two or three characters on it, and the people must recognize them before they can pass.

The villages were different in some ways and yet so much the same. One place we got to and asked the way, but no one would say a word to us. We found a cavalry corps was stationed there and everyone was afraid to give any directions. In most places, the people were burdened by the struggle to live, with heavy taxes added on.

The crop had failed, but they were making a little by spinning cotton and weaving cloth. The food is of the poorest. I would stop to gather the people round. First I would speak of their sorrows and burdens; then I would change; I began to show a world that was burdened – the burden of war; the sorrows, the struggles, the Christian struggle for freedom, and before long they began to forget themselves, and think of the burdens of others the whole world over.

It is wonderful to feel oneself one with the people. I remember, one night, being in a very poor home for supper. The small light was so poor that its rays only lit up the nearby things, and the further parts were just dim objects. There was the faint outline of a spinning loom. All day long they work at it right into the dark hours of the night; click, click, click, it goes all the while. I sat with a bowl of 'chiao tyus'. The man of the house was with me. In the dim light the wife could be seen every now and then attending to the fire and preparing the food. The girl used to come to the evening meetings and I can see those great longing eyes, looking up into my face, so eager, so expectant, just like the child in 'The Light of the World'.

As the meal drew to a close, two young men from next door appeared, with their bowl of gruel. They squatted on the floor and started chatting about English customs and ways of eating. They would laugh and then they asked me to speak in English. Soon we would be on to singing. I'd sing in English and then the same piece in Chinese. I'd teach them in Chinese, and while they sang in Chinese, I'd sing in English and we'd all laugh. And so, for the time being, we forget the sorrows of the present in the laughter of fellowship.

Eric's great secret was that he loved people, and could talk to anyone. The Chinese adored him. They soon found him as useful as a buffer in their quarrels as the mission staff had done in Tientsin. 'Li Mu Shi will settle it,' they would say: 'Ask Li Mu Shi what he thinks about it.'*

Li Mu Shi was also good at sweet-talking the Japanese, whose skirmishes with the Eighth Route Army were signalled daily by the repeated crack of gunfire and the clatter of machine-guns. 'He would reply to savage or shouted queries with a beaming smile and perfect good nature,' said a colleague. 'The Japanese were then indulging in a campaign of petty persecution to try and get rid of the Siaochang missionaries, but against that smiling calm their efforts broke time and again. He was asked to go to military HQ to answer questions, and he cycled off alone to the town, seven miles away. The gendarmerie tried threats, warnings and accusations in vain; Eric remained cheerful but quite firm.'

In order to rejoin his family in Tientsin, he had to pass from Chinese-controlled into Japanese-held territory. Sentries would search his clothes, and even his shoes, looking for secret letters. On one occasion a Japanese sentry stopped him and tried to take his compass from him. 'I told them it was of more value to me than to them,' he explained afterwards. So he was allowed to keep it.

A doctor at the mission hospital said the peacefulness emanating from the hospital even under greatest stress came from something Eric Liddell had taught them:

We have been able to help the wounded of four armies, the Japanese, the Chinese Central Army, the Eighth Route Army and the Chinese Army that is helping itself under the Japanese [he wrote]. The local people are not unanimous as to which of the first three types of armies they prefer, as most people think of their own money and food before their country . . . We have had many visits from troops as they have passed through or used our mission as a base for operations . . . With these visits we usually have a huge rush of refugees from the village. We take all the women and children into the church. It shows that in their mind we stand for a safe refuge, unbroken by the worldly warring outside.

* 'Li' stands for Liddell and 'Mu Shi' means 'pastor'; hence the name means nothing more complicated than 'Pastor Liddell'.

Eric had taught the hospital staff to treat all these soldiers as children of God whom He cared for. To Eric, said the same doctor, there was neither Japanese nor Chinese, soldier nor civilian: they were all men Christ died for.

The disruptions of war were everywhere. Not even a church service could escape the shells. Eric was once preparing to conduct a baptismal service in an outlying area:

The day before for several hours we heard the distant rumble of guns. Sunday dawned, and as we were having breakfast a scouting aeroplane circled above us. Round and round it went, then off, only to come back again. Rumours of an approaching attack were in the air. Our numbers at service were considerably less than we had anticipated, and the people from other villages were absent.

I was in the middle of the address to those receiving baptism when the attack started. The shells exploded with a terrific noise; afterwards we found that two had landed fairly near, one being just round the corner from us. There was a silence for a moment and then we continued . . . No one left the building after the service was over, so we just continued with hymns and witness.

There being no troops here, the Japanese soon entered. There were thirty-one truck-loads of them. They searched every place; they entered the church, but on seeing what it was, left at once, only to pop back a minute later to tell us to get the writing on the outside of the church rubbed off. Their visit was a short one, perhaps four hours in all. Only one person was hurt by an exploding shell. They put up notices in the main street and told the people not to be afraid as they were only out to fight the 'bandits', meaning the Eighth Route Army. They were true to their word; they harmed no one, looted comparatively little, and went.

The suffering Eric saw in those times affected him deeply. Miss Annie Buchan remembers the time he visited a village the Japanese had just left. They had taken one man out of his house for questioning, and when he refused to answer, shot him without more ado. Eric told her afterwards, 'I had nothing to say. I just stood there and then I said, "What could God have done?" ' Miss Buchan, in her eighties, wept as she told me the story. 'He had such sympathy,' she said. 'Never a lot of talk, but you could see it on his face. Always on his face.'

'We constantly had casualties in terrible conditions,' Annie Buchan recalls, 'but there was one especially awful one at Huo Cho. Eric found a man just outside the village. The Japs thought they had beheaded him – he was a stout man of forty – but they hadn't. He had a very deep wide slash round his neck. He had been lying five days like that before they found him.

'Eric was there. I remember Eric's face. On these occasions you just had nothing to say. But the emotion was there on his face. Cry? No, he couldn't afford to cry.

'Mr McColl and Dr Graham, when this man came into the hospital, they took him in and made a very good job of it. He did live. That man became a Christian, and they found he was an artist.'

The man's art-work still hangs in houses all over Edinburgh, because he painted a number of pictures to express his gratitude, and Eric sent copies home as presents. This is how Eric told the story in a letter home:

When journeying back from Tientsin to Siaochang my colleagues and I heard of a wounded man, lying in a temple, twenty miles from our Mission Hospital. No carter would take the risk of taking wounded men, for fear of meeting the Japanese troops on the way. However, one Chinese carter said he would go, if I accompanied him. They have a wonderful confidence in us!!! It would be quite dangerous for him, but I think there was no danger so far as I was concerned.

On Saturday, February 18, the carter started on the journey and some hours later I cycled after him. By evening the carter reached Huo Chu, eighteen miles from Siaochang, where we had our Mission premises. I cycled on to Pei Lin Tyu, three miles further on, to see the Headman of the village and make arrangements for the wounded man to be removed. He lay in the temple about 100 yards outside the village. The temple is a filthy place open to the wind and dust. No one ever comes along to clean it.

No home was open to the wounded man, for if the Japanese descended on them and found that a home had anything to do with the military, it would be destroyed at once, and the lives of those in it would be in danger.

For five days the man had lain in the temple. A friend came there daily to feed him. He lay on a thin mattress on the ground. When we remember that the nights and days are cold and that every night the temperature would be at freezing point, if not well below it, we marvel that he was still alive. The Japanese (a tank and ten motor lorries) were at the next village a mile away.

I told the wounded man we would be back early the next day, and then I returned to Huo Chu. That night, as I lay down, wrapped in my old sheepskin coat, my thoughts turned to the next day. Suppose I met the Japanese, what would I say? I felt for my Chinese New Testament, a book I constantly carried about with me. It fell open at Luke 16. I read until I came to verse 10, and this seemed to me to bring me my answer. 'He that is faithful in that which is least is faithful also in much; and he that is unjust in the least is unjust also in much.' It was as if God had said to me, 'Be honest and straight.' I turned and went to sleep. We started early the next morning. As we approached the first village, there was a man standing in the entrance to it, beckoning us in. We entered the village and as we passed through it the Japanese mechanized troops went round it. We fortunately missed each other.

Many of the roads had been dug up, and were like enlarged trenches, and in clambering out our cart overturned. We reached Pei Lin Tyu early in the day and went to the temple. It was Chinese New Year's Day. People were in the temple burning incense. They were even burning it at the side of the wounded man. I asked the people to come out. I gave them a talk on fresh air being of more value to sick or wounded than air laden with incense smoke. Then I turned to those great words from Micah – 'Wherewith shall I come before the Lord? Shall I come before Him with burnt offerings? . . . He hath shewed thee, O man, what is good; and what doth the Lord require of thee, but to do justly, and to love mercy, and to walk humbly with thy God?'

We laid the man in the cart and left. On reaching Huo Chu, we heard of another man whom we could pick up by going out of our way a short distance. We decided to go and see. When we reached Pang Chuang we went to see the headman. He and some others led us to one of the out-houses. Several men went in first to warn the wounded man that a foreigner was coming in to see him, but that he need not be afraid. On entering I could see, in the dim light, a man reclining on a bed, dirty rags wrapped about his neck. He was one of six men who had been surrounded by the Japanese. They were told to kneel for execution. Five knelt but the sixth remained standing. When the officer came to him he drew his sword and slashed at him, making a gash from the back of his neck to his mouth. He fell as dead. After the Japanese left the villagers came out, and finding him still alive, they had taken him to this out-house where he had lain for several days.

Eric described the bumpy journey to Siaochang Hospital, eighteen miles away, with Japanese planes circling overhead and troops moving parallel to them a mile away. On reaching the hospital, the first man, the one they had found in the temple, died.

No wonder the Eric Liddell story kept ministers in sermon material for months. Who needed the ancient parable of the Good Samaritan when they had the example of Liddell rescuing a dying man in a temple with relentless incense-burners walking past on the other side of the shrine? The parallels were irresistible – right down to the wandering evangelist doing good among the poor, telling stories to simple people, preaching about the Kingdom of Heaven.

But that really was Eric Liddell as Annie Buchan remembers him.

'Oh, he was attractive. His eyes were always shining and he always had a marvellous smile. But he never spoke a lot. He was very quiet. But when he did, he always had something to say. There was just never any doubt that he had this inner power. All the people loved him. It was his kindness and his attitude towards them. He sympathized with them and assured them how much he cared.

' "Eric, how do you really feel?" I asked him once. "Have you any regrets about leaving a city and a college with high-grade students and coming here, trudging round this district in all weathers?" (because the preaching was always done in the open air, you know). Without any hesitation he said, "Never. I have never had so much joy and freedom in my work as here." '

But Tientsin itself was hardly a haven of security. The Japanese had firm control there. There was sporadic guerrilla fighting, and tension in the city was mounting daily. Chinese newspapers had been suppressed and Japanese-controlled papers, printed in Chinese, were thrust into every house with a demand for payment. The British newspaper in Tientsin, which was the main source of information for foreigners in North China, ventured a criticism of the Japanese military and was summarily banned – except in the British and French concessions. The Japanese were in control of transport, railways, the post office and the currency.

The Japanese were flooding the area with heroin to help finance the war effort. Before the war, Eric had watched the heroin-runners in operation between Manchuria and North China. The ticket-collectors on the trains had allowed the pedlars to operate, even in those days of strict Chinese customs control. But now that the Japanese were in charge, drugs were being allowed to pour into China. The cities were also being flooded with cheap Japanese goods.

He was glad to take his family out of it all in the summer of 1939 when he went on his second furlough. He took Florence and the girls to Canada first and left them in Toronto with Florence's mother while he returned to Scotland – and to another round of public acclaim and speaking engagements. Scottish friends noticed that he had grown more serious, and lost even more hair. Britain was now at war, and Eric promptly volunteered to be a pilot in the RAF.

Florence still smiles at the thought. Eric, she says, was such an old romantic. It was just like him to go for something madly dashing, like being a fighter pilot. And dangerous. It had to be the riskiest job going.

But they turned him down flat. At thirty-seven he was too old for flying duties. They offered him a desk job, and you might have thought that, after all he had been through in China, all the heat and flooding and bullet-dodging and separation from his family, he would at least have considered a nice soft job, with a smart uniform and regular leaves with his family. But he replied at once, 'If you're only going to stick me behind a desk, then I've got more important work to do.' Florence and the girls joined him in Edinburgh in March 1940, and five months later they all left for China again.

They nearly didn't make it. Off the Irish Sea their ship – part of a convoy of fifty – was hit by a torpedo.

It was 8.30 p.m. when the children were asleep [Eric wrote later]. Whether it was a 'dud', and only the cap exploded, or whether it had expended its energy, having been fired from too great a distance, or had exploded right below us, we are not sure. I would say that we were actually hit, and that only the cap exploded, judging from the feel in our cabin. No alarm was given for us to go to the boats, but the signal for all boats to zigzag was given by ours.

The next night we lost one of our ships at the back of the convoy. The sea was choppy – a very difficult one to spot submarines in. The escort left us the next day. This was the hardest of all days. About 10 a.m. a small boat about a quarter of a mile from us was torpedoed, blew up, and sank in two minutes; they must have hit the engine boiler. We were on deck ready for the boats, and everyone zigzagged. About noon the 'all-clear' went and we turned to dinner. We had just started, and were half-way through the first course, when the alarm went again. Another boat torpedoed. It didn't sink. We heard later that it was able to get along. Whether it turned back or tried to carry on, I don't know.

We were still in convoy, but not escorted now. By teatime they decided it was too dangerous going on in convoy, so we broke it and each put on full steam ahead . . . It was a tense time right up to the next morning. At 6 p.m. word came through by wireless that the ships which had been sailing next to us, about 200 yards off, for the last two days had been torpedoed. Ten minutes later, another; and at nine o'clock at night we heard that a submarine had risen to the surface and was being engaged by one of the convoy in a running fight.

The ship was running at full speed, far above its average. All night people slept in their clothes, with life-belts ready. The next day the tension eased; we were going out of range of the ordinary submarines; only an ocean-going one could come so far, and there were few of these. The greater speed in the heavy sea caused numbers to be sea-sick again. Since then it has been calmer. No excitement; we have had enough for one trip . . .

Both the kids are well, except that 'Tricia has developed a cough these last two days. They weren't scared at all, for they didn't really know what it all meant. People on board have been very friendly and the crew have been exceptionally helpful. The loss of life in the sinkings would be small. Of the five ships that went down only two were British. They were all cargo boats. It is estimated that if all perished the total wouldn't be more than eighty. Still, eighty means a lot of sadness and suffering!

They made it at last to Nova Scotia, enjoyed a brief rest in Toronto and were back in Tientsin before the end of October 1940. Eric settled his family in the city and returned to the work at Siaochang. The situation there was now much worse. He found Siaochang had become a garrisoned village with a high wall. It looked to Eric, staring out from his bedroom window, like 'one of the outposts of the Empire'. He watched a stream of dejected men going out on forced labour to prepare a motor road to pass to the east of Siaochang.

Ruthlessly land is requisitioned without any compensation [he wrote]. Ancient burial places and graves are disregarded as the Japs gradually force their way further in and drive their roots deeper. It is the people who suffer all along. It makes you think of the old Roman press gangs, and brings with it an ever increasing hatred and rebellious spirit that these things should be.

The Japanese had not had an easy time occupying the district. The Chinese Eighth Route Army was not allowing them to settle. Before and during Eric's furlough, battles were raging round the mission compound. Miss Annie Buchan recalls how one day a Japanese officer called to say that they were going to park their carts and ammunition against the hospital, with twenty soldiers on guard over them. They knew that the Chinese would not fire on the hospital. As the morning wore on the noise of battle came closer, and a Japanese officer estimated that by three o'clock the Eighth Route Army would be routed. But, two hours later, the Japanese were in full retreat, fleeing for their lives.

It was a nerve-racking time. The next day a village near the mission was completely wiped out. Other villages were devastated. Many died, many more were seriously wounded, and once more the casualties poured into the hospital. To make room for them, refugees had to be turned out of the church and housed in the school. The missionaries boiled surgical instruments and changed dressings under the supervision of the hospital staff. And, in the middle of it all, the Japanese arrived and carried out an inspection of the hospital, while the Chinese schoolchildren lined up and bowed a welcome.

Alex Baxter, a young evangelist missionary who was helping in the hospital that day, was disgusted by the refusal of local Chinese leaders to give the missionaries any help: 'We begged for food for our refugees, but they would give neither grain nor a stove to boil grain. Nothing showed more clearly the fundamental, even startling difference between the Christian outlook and the non-Christian. One would have expected them to share something of the heavy burden of the Mission. They had seen us caring for hundreds of their own people. We had cared for hundreds and the mind cannot face the thought of what has happened to the many hundreds more who could not come to us.'

As Liddell continued his pastoral work around the villages, the tension and fear in the air hit him at every turn in the road. When he approached a village he would invariably spot a man lounging on the outskirts, posted there to warn the village of approaching danger. When he went to a church to conduct a wedding, people were too afraid to come out and join him for worship on the eve of the ceremony. He described the wedding:

Saturday was the great day. The bridegroom goes his rounds first thing, paying his respects to all who are related to him or are taking part in the ceremony. At ten o'clock the people had gathered in the church. The bridegroom was there with all the splendour of new clothes, a red sash round his waist and over his shoulder, and a great paper flower on his chest. The bride arrived in a chair and came out at the entrance to the church. It was a cold, windy day, and she looked cold. Although the place was filled, and there were many children present, they were all as quiet as could be during the whole service.

After the bowing was over and the benediction pronounced, we turned and went to where the bridal dinner was prepared. And so, in the midst of all the fears and alarms, the world goes on as if all were calm and quiet. The heavier guns could be heard that evening only a mile away, as they fired in the direction of the people who were cutting up the road. But in Huo Chu we just met together for a service of prayer, praise and thanks, thinking about our contribution to a better world; and the bridal pair spent their first night with the sound of gunfire in their ears, but love and joy in their hearts.

I stayed on over Sunday, taking the service and chatting with the people. I should have returned that day, but the cart I was expecting did not arrive till nightfall. It had been delayed by the Eighth Army, who were stopping the moving of all carts. On our return journey today there was little of incident except at one point. The enemy must have taken us for the Eighth Army and fired two shots. We just got off our bikes and stayed still till they realized their mistake, and then we went on.

My work will be going round the various churches. I now go out to the south-west to a part I have never visited before. When I am out it is giving, giving, all the time, and trying to get to know the people, and trying to leave them a message of encouragement and peace in a time when there is no external peace at all.

By now the missionaries were beginning to realize that their time in Siaochang could be getting short. It was obvious that sooner or later the British in China, hitherto tolerated at least by the Japanese, would be regarded as the enemy, and then their days of freedom would be numbered. The country was in chaos. The war that had started with a patched-up unity between the Nationalists and the Communists and was fought on a united Chinese front against the Japanese, had become a war of two Chinas. The Red Army and the Nationalist army were attacking the invader separately, and at the beginning of 1941 Chiang Kai-shek's government and the Communists stopped talking to each other altogether. Supplies were cut off from Communist armies all over the country. A blockade of government troops was thrown about the Communist civilian base in northern Shensi and it was sealed off. So now the government troops were fighting the Japanese, the Communists were fighting the Japanese and the government troops were fighting the Communists.

In this senseless game, the invading Japanese had a field day, and swarmed all over the country. But they did not have it all their own way. A correspondent writing in 1942 was impressed by the unflinching determination of the exceedingly young Chinese soldiers. Describing what it was like after the Chinese victory over the Japanese in the ten-day battle of Changsha, in central Hunan, he wrote:

And now from everywhere there appeared blue-helmeted soldiers in light blue padded cotton uniforms. They were all young. They walked in the sunlight out of the shelter of bomb holes with an unexpected swagger, their bayonets gleaming. We photographed them. They smiled. They were very eager to talk about the battle, and they mentioned Colonel Li, who had defended the city from within, with extraordinary respect and affection. 'A general or an officer who obtains the respect of his soldiers in China can work miracles,' someone said, and it was easy to believe him, for these youths, fingering their bayonets and gazing dreamily at the passing coffins, are soldiers of whom any country could be proud. They were nearly all Hunanese, fighting for their homes – farmers' lads, mostly, with faces like ripe apples and a gay swing in their movements. All winter they had been waiting. To while the time away, they had planted vegetables on their blockhouses, and it was curious to turn into a side street and see, through a curtain of bayonets, lettuces sprouting above corrugated-iron houses.

We followed the soldiers along a broken street, where the charred buildings were still smoking. Occasionally only a single wooden post would remain standing. A tree stump or a lamp-post with bullet holes was like a wound still bleeding, but those bullet marks on wooden posts were so fresh that they seemed to have been made only a few moments before. Here the nakedness of war appeared in all its violence, for bodies still lay in the houses, and the sound of pickaxes echoed in the still wintry morning. It was strangely quiet . . . High above the city aeroplanes flew and fought in the cold winter sun . . . When they had gone, the city was more silent than ever, until suddenly we heard the sound of squealing pigs and turning a corner we watched three Hunanese peasants wheeling their barrows – with immense centre wheels and curved flanks, which were so delicately carved that they would grace a museum of modern industrial art. The barrows contained children in bright red leggings and woollen mufflers, and their expressions were oddly at variance with the expressions of the peasants, who looked grimed and sad with too much wandering. Behind the peasants came the squealing pigs. The peasants told us that they were going back to their homes on the west bank of the river, and their faces under their black turbans lit with relief when the soldiers gave them a right of way . . .

The Japanese had attempted to gain possession of the burial mound which overlooked the city. From there, with their heavy guns, they could dominate the fortress. And everything in their plans they achieved except that they failed to bring up any heavy guns at all, for the roads were cut by the partisans. They had obeyed the pure theory, and failed to make it a reality. They fought a battle of the imagination, and inevitably they failed.

The year before that battle, Eric and his colleagues had been forced to evacuate the mission compound at Siaochang. They had known for weeks it was coming, for they had sensed the attitude of the Japanese changing. At the beginning of the war the invaders had treated the British with a measure of civility – they might have wandered through the hospital sticking their swords into the dressings, but Annie Buchan was in charge and she knew how to put them in their place. Now the soldiers started coming into their homes, drunk and brandishing their swords. One day Annie Buchan rushed into the hospital operating theatre, looking urgently for a doctor, and found a soldier had pinned the doctor against the wall and was hitting him with his baton. She marched up, grabbed the doctor and said, 'I want this doctor.' The soldier fell back in sheer astonishment. It was clear to her that there had been a shift in authority: the officers no longer made any effort to control their men.

Early in 1941, the missionaries were told to pack their bags and get out. They had two weeks to get ready, but were then told they could take nothing with them. They handed over the keys of their house to the Japanese and left, along the road to the railway station on their last journey to Tientsin. They heard later that Siaochang had been destroyed – every last brick and plank of it.

While all that was going on, Eric had been growing increasingly worried for the safety of his family in Tientsin. Was it right to keep them in Tientsin when the British were liable to be interned at any time? Patricia and Heather were still toddlers and Florence was expecting another baby. The decision, taken with the board of the missionary society, was that they should leave for the safety of Canada.

'It was a very difficult decision,' Florence recalls. 'I didn't want to come away at all. But we were sure Japan was going to come into the Second World War. Eric could have come with us, but he didn't feel he should. He said he would feel so much better if I had the children in Canada. He was worried that if they took us hostage, he didn't think he could trust himself. No, I never felt his work came first. It wasn't like that at all. He just felt others were staying and he ought to as well.'

Did the thought flit across Eric's mind when he said good-bye to them all that he might not see them again? It certainly never occurred to Florence.

'It just never crossed my mind for a minute. I thought it would be one or two years. Even right at the end it never crossed my mind that anything could happen to Eric. I don't know how I could have been so naive.'

9

'Days of Perplexity Like the Present'

Florence Liddell and the two children set sail for Canada in May 1941, and in September of that year Eric received a telegram telling him of the birth of his third daughter, Maureen – the child he was never to see.

By this time he was living in Tientsin again, sharing a flat in the French concession with Mr A. P. Cullen, who had been one of the schoolmasters at Eltham College during Eric's schooldays there and latterly a senior colleague on the staff of the Tientsin Anglo-Chinese College (he was later to write the biography of *Lavington Hart of Tientsin*, and an edifying book called *Making China's Men*).

For the first time in his experience, Eric Liddell had nothing specific to do, no definite job; but he kept busy. He worked on a *Manual of Christian Discipleship*, which he hoped would be translated into Chinese for the guidance of Chinese pastors. It included sixty pages of Bible readings, with comments for every day of the year. He spent long hours working on that project; but he never deviated from the practice that had become his routine, of rising early and hallowing the 'Silent Hour' which shaped the rest of his day.

There is something about Eric Liddell's 'Silent Hour', something about his self-discipline, about his ideal of the mind, body and spirit working together in obedience to God, which is strongly reminiscent of the Buchmanite Oxford Group, that remarkable evangelistic movement that seized the hearts of so many young students in the 1920s and 1930s. The basic theology of the Oxford Group, in simplified form, was that an individual should confess his sins, accept Jesus Christ as his personal saviour, and share his experience with others whose lives had been changed in this way. It emphasized, indeed demanded, four cardinal principles – moral absolutes – of honesty, purity, unselfishness and love, reinforced by compulsory public 'sharings'. Frank Buchman, the American evangelist who founded the 'Group movement' and was later to become associated with the much more politically orientated 'Moral Rearmament', had been on an evangelistic mission to China in 1918, where he had held the first of the group's famous house parties. All kinds of people were in close session for two weeks – missionaries, pastors, statesmen, businessmen, professional men; it could be that Eric Liddell's missionary father also attended, in which case he may have conveyed something of the excitement of the new movement to his teenage son.

There is no direct evidence that Eric himself was ever a member of the group, or even expressed any interest in it as a movement. But his elder brother Rob had come into contact with it, according to Annie Buchan, who worked with Rob at the Siaochang Mission Hospital. He and another missionary, William F. Rowlands (author of *The Plain and the People*), who was one of the stalwarts of Siaochang, came back from furlough with their wives and started holding confessional group sessions at the mission. Annie Buchan didn't like it.

'I had read Buchman's book and I liked it very much; but when two missionary families come back to a small community and set up a special group, to me it's a bit fishy. I went to their meetings and I found the "confessionals" not to my liking. I said to Will Rowlands one day, "If we're going to have meetings the Chinese can't come to, we're making a division." I said I wouldn't come to the "confessionals" again. And because I wouldn't go, the rest of the hospital staff wouldn't go either.'

This difference of opinion (it would be too strong to call it a split) happened long before Eric was posted to Siaochang. 'Eric wasn't in it,' says Miss Buchan, 'and we never discussed it. I think by then everyone had realized that we couldn't afford a split. The "Inner Circle" disappeared. Eric was not, to my knowledge, ever a member of the inner circle. It was mostly over before he came, but some of it would have suited him; their principles were very good. From my point of view, the problem was the "confessionals"; to me it was a break in our fellowship.'

From all accounts of his attitude to life and faith, Eric Liddell might have been attracted by the Oxford Group's emphasis on spiritual discipline, but the dangerous tendency towards spiritual elitism, as shown in the inner circle of confessionals at Siaochang (at least, as Miss Buchan interprets them), would have had no appeal for him. Eric Liddell was a good listener but a diffident speaker. He wasn't one to bare his soul in front of a crowd. Nor was he ever exclusive. He could never have been attracted to any clique that excluded his flock, the Chinese. His was a much more simple, living Christianity.

Another friend, the Rev. Howard Smith, a Methodist missionary in the English concession in Tientsin with whom Eric would later take refuge, wrote: 'I do not know how or when Eric was influenced by the Oxford Group. Upon his life this movement had only a good effect, for it deepened and strengthened what was already there . . . Eric was applying to all he did and said the "Four Standards"; but he did not do it openly or blatantly. You just knew that those standards were there, always, as an undertone to all he did.'

These months in Tientsin must have been a desperately frustrating period for Eric, when he felt he didn't have anything positive or constructive to do. His life changed drastically, however, in December 1941 – like the lives of millions of others – when the Japanese launched their airborne assault on Pearl Harbor in the Pacific. Within weeks the members of the London Missionary Society were ordered to leave their homes within the French concession. Eric Liddell and six other missionaries were taken into the hospitable homes of members of the English Methodist Mission in the British concession, where they would stay for over a year. They were free to move about the streets, wearing armbands to display their nationality; but they were not allowed outside the concession.

Many of Eric's colleagues really felt at a loose end, but Eric managed to keep himself busy. The Japanese would not permit any assemblies of more than ten people, which effectively put an end to church services. But Eric thought up the idea of a rota of reverends who would prepare a sermon, in turn, for each Sunday; the wives would then invite guests to tea on Sunday afternoons, making sure that each individual company never numbered more than ten. Sufficient copies of the sermon would be run off to ensure that each tea-party was able to have a short service round the tea-table, and the sermons were handed round with the tea-cakes.

This period of comparative inaction must have been a strain for a man whose whole urge was to be up and doing. He played cricket with the sons of the Methodist staff; he taught tennis to their daughters in the blazing heat; he made up fours for bridge. He once queued up for bread at 5 a.m. for his host's family, and got up at the crack of dawn another morning to sweep the house from top to bottom after a dust storm. He wrote long letters to Florence and eagerly read her news of the children's progress. How he longed to see his new baby!

D. P. Thomson cites a letter from Eric at this time, showing that he was thinking of applying for repatriation. Everyone was asked to sign a form saying whether or not he wanted to stay; Eric had wanted to remain, but then so many others decided to do the same thing that he felt he could perhaps be spared to do more useful work elsewhere than he was doing in China. He wrote to ask Florence what she thought about the idea of a Home Mission in Canada. He felt that the need out there was great, and if he got back he might like to have a crack at it.

The fate of the missionaries in China was not exactly front-page news in a Britain that was being bombed and was fighting across half the world. China, being the enemy of Japan, was now our ally and Madame Chiang Kai-shek's fund-raising tours were brought to the notice of the public, who added 'Aid to China' to their list of flag days. London Missionary Society magazines and reports were the only publications that relatives could scan for some hint of what was happening to people like Eric Liddell. They were full of items like the following, taken from *China's Millions*, the magazine of the China Inland Mission:

- ... We must remind our friends that we are no longer allowed to transmit personal gifts to missionaries in China as in pre-war days.

- ... At the present moment no British women are allowed to sail for 'occupied' China, and we have to suspend, just for the moment, the training of women recruits.

- ... When the Japanese occupied Changtze, where Miss Lundgren and Miss Bachmann were stationed, the ladies were cut off from all supplies and lived for four months on a diet of millet porridge three times a day ... Miss Bachmann's health – she had been suffering from digestive trouble – greatly improved. It is interesting to hear that an American Mission doctor in Peking has discovered the virtues of millet porridge for digestive trouble and now gives it a regular place on her own menu, and feeds her friends on it, too.

- ... After Mr Kenneth Price had escorted his wife to Siaochang for medical attention and returned to Kienteh, the Japanese attack and capture of Siaochang took place. So Mr Price is now separated from his wife, he still in Free China and she in Japanese-occupied territory.

- ... One of the senior Japanese officers in Kaifeng ... has been very friendly during the last few weeks as a result of Dr Hess having located, by means of the hospital X-ray machine, a bullet which had lodged in his chest. He has since brought his wife along for medical treatment.

- ... It is encouraging to note that in days of perplexity like the present, the leaders of our Mission in China are not contemplating retreat, or withdrawal, but are even planning for advance.

- ... The last foreign missionary has been driven out of Turkestan.

- ... Deaths: At Siakiang, Mrs H. Sames, from bombing injury; at Tachu, Szechwan, Esther Grace Simmonds, aged 10½ months, from dysentery; at Chengku, Mr Arnold Strange, of typhus; at Chefoo, Frank Sidney Barling, from typhoid fever.

- ... It would be difficult to exaggerate the gravity of the situation in the Far East ... Many of our friends will feel deep concern about the staff and the children in the Chefoo schools.

- ... Every bed in the hospital is filled. There is a waiting list of drug addicts. I took in the fifty-eighth today.

- ... The Japanese erected electrified barricades around the British concession in Tientsin, stationing sentries and police at the various entrances and exits.

- ... *The Generalissimo* [Chiang Kai-shek], speaking in Chunking to a missionary group, said: 'We still need and welcome Christians from other lands who will serve the people. Do not feel that you are guests. You are comrades working with us to serve and save our people and to build a new nation.'

- ... Mme Chiang Kai-shek, when speaking to members of the American Bible Society, during her visit to USA, stated that she and the Generalissimo had arranged that Chinese scholars make a new translation of the Psalms, which had been completed, and of the New Testament, which was in process of translation.

- ... The Chinese ambassador to the United States, a Buddhist, said recently: 'As an unreconstructed heathen I wish to pay my respects to all the Christian missionary workers who have aided China during these years of her struggle. Many of these missionaries have lost their property, have suffered physical injury. Their women have suffered grave indignities, physical hardships and misery, but so far as I know, no missionary has deserted his post.'

- ... From Mr and Mrs Crane, on the Burma Border: 'The fight was on ... We wasted a morning packing for flight. Then, as the next morning greeted us with still more livid flames from a third village burning, we wasted a second hour or so discussing where to flee, and then, as everything had continued quiet, we wasted a third hour unpacking to stay!'

- ... *The Chefoo Schools*. The entire schools have been interned by the Japanese together with all other foreign residents, in the compound of the American Presbyterian Mission in Chefoo. No further news has since been received ... We understand that the Japanese marched into the schools and took possession of a section of the premises on August 27th and pressed for the complete evacuation of the whole building.

- ... *Famine Conditions*. Our readers will doubtless have seen in the press reference to the appalling famine conditions affecting many millions in a part of the Province of Honan. We understand that thousands have been dying of starvation. It is reported that Madame Chiang has allocated a substantial amount to famine relief from the gift she has received through Lady Cripps' Fund ... If any feel constrained to do something for the relief of these stricken people they can send their contribution to . . . British Fund for the Relief of Distress in China.

- . . . *Madame Chiang Kai-shek*. It will be known that this noble Christian lady is now in the United States for medical treatment, and prayer should be offered on her behalf for a complete and speedy recovery. It has been rumoured that Madame Chiang will visit this country after her stay in the USA . . . It was deeply interesting to notice that in allocating funds . . . Madame Chiang gave a large proportion of the money to Christian enterprises.

- . . . *Sino-British Friendship*. We heartily welcome the cordial and friendly relationship which exists between the rulers and people of China and ourselves . . . The record of our dealings with China in years gone by has not been what we could have wished, but there is evidently a sincere desire on the part of our rulers to express sympathy with China in her present difficulties and future aspirations. The proposal to abandon all extra-territorial rights in China is an evidence of this, and is a move in the right direction.

- . . . *The British Red Cross Unit* . . . has now taken up its quarters in the Bible Institute at Changsha in Hunan.

- . . . *Missionaries in Occupied China*. News has come to us that all the British and Americans in Shanghai, Tientsin and Tsingtao were being interned . . . A cablegram informs us that the following missionaries were interned in Yangchow, where one of the camps established by the Japanese is situated. It is probably the Women's Language School of the CIM in which they are interned: Mr and Mrs A. L. Keeble, Millin, Price, Scott, Weller, Fleischmann, Hayman . . .

- . . . *The Problem of finance in China*. One of the serious difficulties . . . is the continuing and uncontrolled soaring of prices of all necessities, and the situation is aggravated by the Chinese having 'pegged' the exchange for sterling at 80 dollars to the £1. A more just exchange would probably be ten times as much . . . Recent letters state that in Chunking a suit of clothes costs £60 to £70, a pair of socks £5, potatoes 1s 2d a lb. Wages of servants are now so fantastically high to make it virtually impossible to employ any.

- . . . Through the kind offices of the Minister of Finance it has been arranged that money sent out for missions and for philanthropic purposes shall receive a bonus of fifty per cent on the exchange . . . but this is rather nullified by the still higher rise in prices.

- ... A missionary doctor, Catherine Simmons, described the famine in Honan Province:

  'Military grain taxes have been getting heavier and heavier, and ever since I have been in Honan strings of carts have been streaming out of the Province, loaded with military wheat. So there were no reserves. Then last year's wheat was a very poor crop. The summer following was the longest, hottest, driest known for over thirty years at least, and most of the autumn crops of sweet potatoes, beans, etc., perished in the drought.

  'I was in Western Glory [Sihwa] through the summer, and Joel describes, far better than I could ever hope to, what we saw there when the locusts came. On streamed the unbroken ranks, set in battle array. It was not exactly the garden of Eden before them, but at least there were the remnants of the autumn crop that had survived the drought, and on which so much hope was set, but behind them was a desolate wilderness – the bare, brown land stripped of every vestige of green.

  'The city's gods were carried out to bake in the sunshine, and day and night gongs and drums were beaten before them as prayers were made to the powers of evil to possess a man so that he might prophesy when rain would come ... The urgent need for rain was that next year's wheat might be planted; only a month to planting time; only three weeks; only two – and then the dykes of the Yellow River gave way and the waters swept over the plain, right into the outskirts of the city, and the last hope of planting wheat was gone!

  'These last months of winter have been the worst, and some could not face them, so had one last, tasty meal, the last mouthful of which was so prepared that next day they wouldn't have to worry about food ...'

- ... *Interned Missionaries.* Not much news is reaching us from our friends who are interned, but from what little information has come out ... the spirit and cheerful courage displayed is deeply moving and impressive. ... There is still some hope that there may be a small repatriation of a small number of internees ...

- ... *From a missionary in West Yunnan.* Arrival of Superintendent from a journey to the Salween River to try to get in touch with the Hattons who were cut off by the Jap advance last year. He was unsuccessful ... but we found he had with him a young American pilot who had to bale out of his plane after getting his oil pipe hit by a stray Jap bullet fired from the ground ... Hattons arrived here two days ago, safe and well!

- *. . . Report from Yangchow.* We saw first-hand something of the methods used by the invader toward a conquered people – economic pressure to the point where they can hardly exist because of high prices on one hand, and acute shortage of necessities on the other – in short, terrorism and despotism: the most insidious method used to undermine the morale is the introduction of narcotics – opium, heroin, to which thousands are falling victims.

- *. . . Health Services in China.* It has been computed that each day there are 16 million sick persons in China; the yearly death roll is 10 million, of whom 4 million need not die if adequate medical attention were available. It would probably be true to say that the organization of present health services in China is largely due to the work of the medical missionary in former years. Whatever might be the estimate in which medical missionary service is held by people at home, the Chinese are more than ever convinced, especially through their experiences during the war years, that missionaries have a genuine love for the people themselves.

- *. . . Interned Missionaries.* Messages from the internment camps indicate that living conditions are tolerable . . . From a repatriated missionary comes news of . . . the Boys' School recently removed from Chefoo to Weihsien, where there are 2000 Allied nationals interned. The Japanese were said to be acting towards the children with consideration.

- *. . . Stop Press.* We deeply regret to have to record the death of Mrs Hoyte, wife of Dr Stanley Hoyte, at Lanchow on December 19th from typhus. (Mrs Hoyte had left her six children with the Principal of the school at Chefoo to join her husband at Kansu in 1940.)

- *. . . Weihsien.* Our latest news reads, 'We are living a peaceful happy healthful life . . .'

- *. . . Freed.* One of the Chefoo School boys, recently repatriated writes: . . . 'I have gained 25 lbs since I left China . . .'

By the end of 1942 the flow of news from China was down to a trickle. From the occupied zone in the north-east letters had virtually stopped coming. The Japanese were tightening their grip on the Europeans in Tientsin, and Eric Liddell and his colleagues were speculating as to whether they would be repatriated, or deported or worse. The strongest rumour was that they would be taken from Tientsin to an internment camp.

10

'It's Complete Surrender . . .'

When you hear that Eric Liddell died in a Japanese internment camp on 21 February 1945, you immediately think of brutality and beatings and starvation, and a heroic death in the face of dirt and disease and inhuman cruelty – the way that so many thousands of ordinary men and women met their end in the Far East in those terrible years. But it wasn't like that for Eric Liddell. And this very fact makes the story of his death, paradoxically, all the more moving.

If he had fallen to a Japanese bayonet or a Samurai sword, or if he had stopped one of the bullets he had managed to dodge in the no-man's-land around Siaochang, or if he had even died of straight hunger at Weihsien internment camp, it would have fitted in much better with the romantic image that the public had bestowed on him since that distant day of glory at the Paris Olympics. Yet, after nearly forty years, the manner of Eric Liddell's dying is still poignant, simply because it was so untheatrical, so real, so down-to-earth – as the man himself had always been.

He died as most folk do, because something had gone desperately wrong with the chemistry of his body. He fell prey to a fatal disease, but its effects were slow, and painful, and remained unrecognized as such; and although he bore the excruciating pain with the same gritty determination he had always displayed on the race-track, the irony is that the disease came to affect the aspect of him that had always been his strength and his main attraction, the one attribute that had enabled him to move men and mountains. And that was his personality itself.

It wasn't that he changed from a sunny-natured optimist into a disagreeable curmudgeon – he remained kind and considerate to others right to the end. But he fell victim to bouts of depression that were totally alien to the real Eric Liddell, and which made him feel a failure to the faith that had always buttressed him.

But a 'failure' was the last thing he would be called, even at the end. Especially at the end.

On 12 March 1943, Eric Liddell and his colleagues in Tientsin got the call – along with hundreds of other British, American and assorted 'enemy nationals' – to go to the Civil Assembly Centre at Weihsien in Shantung Province, just to the south of Peking. Ever since the attack on Pearl Harbor in December 1941 and America's full-scale entry into the Second World War, it had only been a matter of time before the foreigners in Japanese-occupied China would be interned. Luckily, since no resistance had been offered to the Japanese in Peking or Tientsin, they were to be classified not as prisoners of war but as 'civil internees'.

The British were to go in three parties, and Eric was appointed captain of the missionaries' group in the third party. They were given until 26 March to send their luggage ahead; each was allowed four pieces – three trunks, and his bed and bedding. Two suitcases could be carried as hand luggage on the journey, which enabled them to take a good many personal effects along. But nobody warned them that eating utensils would have been useful, too.

On 30 March they assembled at 7.30 p.m. and their luggage was inspected by the Japanese guards. Two hours later they marched off down the streets of Tientsin to the railway station. Allied personnel from all over North China had been rounded up in this way, and in both Peking and Tientsin the spectacle was the same: hundreds of British and Americans of all ages and all backgrounds were struggling along the streets with their luggage.

Sympathetic Chinese onlookers lined the streets to see them go. It was stage-managed by the Japanese as a spectacle of humiliation.

They were bundled into third-class railway carriages, missionaries and businessmen, society ladies and prostitutes, nurses and secretaries, all together. At 11.40 p.m. their train moved out, and most of the passengers sat up all night. They changed trains at Tainan next morning, and arrived at Weihsien at 3.40 in the afternoon. The camp was about two miles from the city.

The compound was small, only about 150 by 200 yards: very small for 1,800 people to live in. Ironically, it was a ruined American Presbyterian mission station, grey and institutional like all the foreign mission stations. Its Chinese name meant 'The Courtyard of the Happy Way'. As the internees straggled in, they noticed a school, a hospital and a church. Some might have been observant enough to spot three kitchens and some bakery ovens. What everyone did notice was that the place was wrecked. The buildings themselves were undamaged, but the insides were a shambles: the contents had been thrown on to the streets, which were strewn with old beds and radiators and bits of piping and broken desks and classroom chairs.

The newcomers were led to their quarters. Unattached men and women went to dormitories; married couples and their children found themselves in rooms measuring 13 by 9 feet. In countless rows of these small rooms all round the camp, families were trying to sort themselves out that night, to the inevitable accompaniment of children's tears.

Sooner or later that first evening, the new internees felt called upon to go and inspect the camp's toilet arrangements. The shock they received has stayed with them to this day. Langdon Gilkey, until then a young instructor at Yenching Anglo-American University near Peking, one of the 'Christian Colleges' in China, describes his first impressions in the book he wrote after it was all over, *Shantung Compound: The Story of Men and Women under Pressure* (1966):

As we entered the door of the Men's Room, the stench of what assailed our Western nostrils almost drove us back into the fresh March air. To our surprise, we found the brand-new fixtures inside: Oriental-style toilets with porcelain bowls sunk into the floor, over which we uncomfortably had to squat. Above them on the wall hung porcelain flushing boxes with long metal pull-chains, but – the pipes from the water tower outside led only into the men's showers; not one was connected with the toilets. Those fancy pipes above us led nowhere. The toilet bowls were already filled to overflowing. With no servants, no plumbers and no running water anywhere in camp, it was hard to see how they would ever be unstopped.

Their depression mounted as they were led to another part of the compound for supper:

I saw stretching before me for some seventy yards, a line of quiet, grim people standing patiently with bowls and spoons in their hands . . . Could human patience bear such a long wait three times a day for meals? However, I joined the line, and three quarters of an hour later we reached the table where thin soup was being ladled out with bread. That was supper. Fortunately there were 'seconds' of bread, because we were very hungry after our long train trip without food.

Our meal finished, we lined up again to have our bowls and spoons washed by women from Tsingtao. The patterns of chores in the new situation were beginning to come clear. As I went out past the steam-filled kitchen with its great Chinese cauldrons, I saw three men from our Peking group being shown how to use the cooking equipment by the men from Tsingtao, turned into 'experts' by their three days of practice.

Before many days were out they were all becoming practised. Society ladies who had scarcely seen the inside of a kitchen before had to scrub floors and wash dishes. There was bread to be baked and water to be drawn; the interior of the compound had to be rebuilt, the meals cooked, the walls mended, the fires stoked, the furniture restored. 'Thus,' wrote Gilkey, 'bank clerks, professors, salesmen, missionaries, importers and executives became bakers, stokers, cooks, carpenters, masons, and hospital orderlies.'

Administration went ahead with typical Japanese efficiency. The camp was divided into three groups, according to their origin in Tientsin, Peking or Tsingtao. Each group ate its meals together in a large dining-room at long wooden tables. Each person had to supply his own cup, plate and cutlery.

Nine departments were set up to co-ordinate camp duties: Discipline; Education, Entertainment and Athletics; Employment; Quarters and Accommodation; and Supplies. Each department had its own committee. There were also the Christian Fellowship of the Protestant Churches, the Women's Auxiliary and the Homes Committee (to help women in their homes). The Employment Committee called for a minimum of three hours' work each day from every medically fit man and woman in the camp. There was no Chinese labour to do the menial duties; every single job had to be done by internees.

They gradually settled into a rhythm. Everybody would get up on the dot of 7 a.m. and attend to the chores. It might be drawing water from the well or sweeping up coal-dust to make into brickettes for heating. Men who once had owned coal-mines had to scrabble on their hands and knees for that coal-dust. It was mixed with earth and put into tubes made from the tins of baby-milk that the Red Cross brought in from the Swiss Embassy. These were left to dry and then became fuel. Old people and invalids relied on others considerate enough to do their chores.

The internees were not officially 'prisoners', so there was generally little harassment by the guards. But twice-daily roll-calls – whatever the weather and whatever your occupation at the time – tried everyone's nerves. Food was in short supply, and people were soon looking thin and wan. They were always hungry.

A Canadian missionary at the camp, sent this account to D. P. Thomson:

After the first month, English-language newspapers were delivered once a week. They were printed in Peking or Japan, and carried only German and Japanese news dispatches but gave a fair representation of the war situation in Europe, and one could usually infer what was the course of events in the Pacific. Every major event was heralded as a Japanese victory! But does a victorious army always retreat?

Before going to camp, American and British nationals who had run out of funds were able to obtain a monthly living allowance loan from their home government through the Swiss representative. This was paid in advance to the end of April. In camp, we could receive on application a 'comfort allowance' of about one tenth of the living allowance. In this way we were not without funds. There were regulations, of course. The money was paid to the commandant and released to us at his discretion, but we received some consideration.

For a nondescript population of 1,800 of several nationalities and various religious and irreligious persuasions, whose liberties were curtailed, it is obvious that some clashes with the guards would be likely, but these were rare and there were no serious developments. Fortunately there were no attempts to escape – such an attempt would probably have failed and undoubtedly would have brought punishment to those who remained, and a more rigid discipline. There was an intermittent over-the-wall black market where many things were purchased – everything from eggs to opium . . .

After the first six weeks the authorities opened a canteen where a very limited stock was on sale. There we could occasionally purchase peanuts, peanut oil, eggs, candy, honey, fruit in season, toothpaste, shoe polish, Chinese shoes and clogs, and a variety of other things. The work of the canteen was done by our own people.

As they settled down, the internees began to organize their own entertainment programmes. First, these were put on once a week, then twice a week in response to popular demand. There were plays, revues, choral programmes, even symphony concerts. On one occasion the audience was treated to Handel's *Messiah*, another time to a full performance of Mozart's Concerto in D Minor (minus double basses and tuba). The culmination of the dramatic enterprises was a full-scale performance of Shaw's *Androcles and the Lion*. It was staged, according to Langdon Gilkey, 'with three complete sets, a full-sized lion made of cloth, cardboard, and armour and helmets for ten Roman guards soldered together out of tin cans from the Red Cross parcels'.

On Sundays there was a variety of church services, with hymn singing in the evening. They even had their own Salvation Army band to play hymns in an open square on Sunday mornings, followed by requests, and an hour's playing outside the hospital. Boy Scouts and Girl Guides continued to meet, and the diligent ones were awarded special 'Weihsien' badges. There were more than a hundred adult education classes on offer in various subjects, including religion, mathematics, painting and philosophy, though there were few takers. The professional teachers banded together to provide a school for the children.

There were hundreds of children in the camp. About 300 had come from the Chefoo school run by the China Inland Mission in the port of Chefoo in Shantung, 500 miles north of Shanghai. It was a school for the children of missionaries. 'Situated on the curve of a quiet bay with a yellow sea-front and a range of hills behind it,' one described it later. 'In a land of famine, poverty, banditry, civil wars and floods, it was a haven of peace for generations of missionaries' children.' It was run as a British public school, with cricket, football, hockey, rowing and tennis.

Both the town of Chefoo and the school had been captured by the Japanese in 1938. A flurry of lorries, a flash of gun-boats in the harbour, and the job was done. Chefoo school settled down again into its old rhythm. In August 1941 most of the children left for home, but that still left many behind. As the Japanese pushed inland and anti-British feeling intensified, the school leaders began to discuss the possibility of evacuating before Britain and the USA were directly involved in the Far East war. But the mission leaders were asked not to organize a mass exodus which would panic the Chinese public. Then came Pearl Harbor, and in 1942 the children moved to the American Presbyterian Mission at Temple Hill to the west of the city. Their next move was to Weihsien internment camp, where they arrived in September 1943, six months after Eric Liddell.

Imagine, then, what life was like at Weihsien. It was an over-populated camp where the only privacy anyone had was an area of 9 feet by 54 inches round his bed; a place peopled by bored children and frustrated teenagers and confused old people, by the widest range of personalities, all rubbing up against each other, queuing for the toilets and the meals and the roll-call and the chores: nerves grinding and personalities clashing, and nowhere to escape to. All the familiar creature comforts were gone, all the structures by which people organize their lives had been turned upside down.

It was hardly surprising, then, that there were tensions; and one of the most marked of the dissonances was between the businessmen and the missionaries. Langdon Gilkey suggests that there had developed in the Far East 'a chasm of distrust and contempt between merchant and missionary', which was thrown into sharp relief when the two groups found themselves stuck in the same compound for years.

'Most of the Westerners in China detested the missionary, and never were able to speak of him except in scorn or ridicule.'

To the missionary, on the other hand, the Western lay businessman was 'hard, immoral, addicted to drink, interested only in mulcting wealth from the poor Chinese while arrogantly excluding them from his cities, clubs and vacation spots, and remaining indifferent to both the values and the needs of their indigenous culture'. There were certain elements of truth here, he says, but the picture was wildly exaggerated. The businessman had simply built his own world which he never left; it never seemed to have crossed his mind that he might become part of the wider Chinese culture around him.

His life was circumscribed by the narrow confines of the business office, the club porch, and the social life among the treaty-port elite. Outside that small circle of foreign equals, there were for him only the Chinese subordinates in his office (whom he did not understand, and so tended to distrust), and beyond them the great sea of Chinese 'natives' in whom he had little interest except as a market. In his environment – 'a little bit of Surrey in North China, old boy' – there was no wider community within which he might, as he would at home, adopt a responsible role commensurate with his wealth and advantages.

The merchants' picture of the missionary was the usual stereotype. To the businessman, says Gilkey the missionary was a loveless, sexless, viceless, disapproving and hypocritical fanatic. He was repressed and repressive, trying to force others into the narrow straitjacket of his own list of rigid 'dos' and 'don'ts' and thus squeezing out of his own life and out of theirs all its natural and redeeming joys. And Gilkey adds:

At first, in Peking, I found this picture incredible; it seemed so clearly not to fit the liberal group I knew. But acquaintance in camp with a much wider circle of missionaries showed that it did contain some truth.

In page after page of Gilkey's account, the missionaries

feature in the most unattractive light. He describes how, at the beginning of the camp, the Japanese had put some of the families of four into two rooms, while others were squashed into one room. In an attempt to give the one-roomed families more space, it was suggested that the teenage children of four-person families could be put into a dormitory. With this in mind, Gilkey visited a prominent American missionary family, who had two sons aged sixteen and thirteen, to ask if one or both of the sons might move into a dormitory, thus providing extra room to help the crowded families. The family must have known about the problem, he says, because one of the overcrowded families of four-in-a-room lived right next door.

'We have had our evening of thought and prayer about the problem you shared with us,' said the missionary's wife, smiling, 'and we have reached our decision. We cannot allow our young sons to go into the dorm.'

'But they will be only 50 yards away!' said Gilkey. 'Surely you don't think anything will happen to them there?'

'Oh no, it's just that Paul is only sixteen and subject to so many influences right now. I don't want to say anything about those other boys, but you know how they are! And besides, the heating and draughts here are very unusual and I know that, with the little he gets to eat, unless someone watches over him, he will always be getting colds and flu. And it is quite out of the question for Johnny at thirteen to leave us.'

'OK, fair enough,' said Gilkey. 'Let's look at another alternative then. How about your youngest moving into this room with you, and Paul moving in with the two Jones boys in the next block?'

'Oh no, we talked about that, too, and have made up our minds. We believe in keeping a nice home for our boys to come to, and that would be impossible with four in one room. As we talked last night, all this became clearer and clearer: home and family are so important in a place like this. We decided that our first moral responsibility in the camp is to keep a real American home for our two boys.'

Gilkey also reports incidents like the squabble between a fervent missionary and a chic British secretary. 'These ruddy missionaries,' the representative of the secretaries explained, 'insisted not only on praying aloud at night, but on singing hymns when they awoke each morning, God help them, at 6 a.m.! We finally got damn well tired of this nonsense, and *that* is the cause of the fight.'

'You know perfectly well it isn't,' retorted an outraged British missionary woman. '*They* insisted on chattering endlessly at night in loud whispers when we were trying to sleep, as any normal woman should have been. And not only talking, but talking about all the lurid escapades in their pasts – half of which I am sure were imagined! And *that* started the fight.'

As a partial solution, the most vociferous hymn-singer was moved into a predominantly missionary dormitory. Annie Buchan, the matron from the Siaochang Mission Hospital who arrived in the camp some months later than the others, remembers a similar type of situation.

'In our dorm there was an old woman, a dear soul. It didn't matter what was happening, her devotions came first. Every morning she would get on her knees on the floor for her devotions. But the person in the next bed had to climb over her to get to her work. That kind of thing went on.' And Annie Buchan chuckles. 'It wasn't really necessary to irritate anyone in your devotions. You could just as easily communicate with God in your own bed.'

Gilkey's catalogue of the unattractive behaviour of the missionaries is relentless. He describes how sixteen packets of American cigarettes arrived once in the parcel each person received from the Red Cross. The missionaries were thus faced with the moral problem of what to do with them. Their rigid principle of non-smoking required that they should destroy the cigarettes, but, Gilkey reports: 'It was very tempting to use them . . . Lucrative deals were now possible, since heavy smokers offered tins of milk, butter, and meat in exchange for a pack or two.' He says that almost all those missionaries who had previously refused to lend out their ration cards now exchanged their sixteen packets of cigarettes for tins of milk or meat.

And Gilkey comments:

It had long been evident that our community was faced with moral problems deep enough to threaten its very existence. And yet a significantly large group of Christian leaders was concerned exclusively with moral issues and vices not connected with these deeper problems of our life. For this reason their very moral intensity tended to make both themselves, and the serious morality which they represented, seem to be a socially irrelevant segment of life rather than the creative force they might have been. The constructive moral forces in our life were only weakened, and the cynical forces strengthened, when missionaries judged honest, hard-working and generally self-sacrificing men as 'weak' – and even went so far as to warn their young people not to associate with them, because they smoked or swore.

In his graphic and disillusioned portraits of the people he remembered, Gilkey used assumed names that are just close enough to the real ones to reveal their true identities. There is scarcely a break in the dismal litany of bickerings and fights and repressive morality and greedy self-seeking. How and where, you begin to wonder, did Eric Liddell fit into all this? These were his people that Gilkey was describing, after all, with hardly anywhere a good word.

Gilkey moves on to the children of non-missionary parents. Life in camp was grey and boring for them. Youngsters in their early teens wandered round the camp at night with nothing to do, and there were rumours of sex orgies in a disused basement. The parents, says Gilkey, became irate at a mass meeting to discuss this crisis, and declared that 'they', whoever that might be, should do something about it. But not one parent offered any concrete suggestions or constructive help, and it was left to the missionary teachers to suggest a solution. It is at that point in Gilkey's decidedly jaundiced account – in which praise is always hedged with reservations and enthusiasm tempered by wariness – that you suddenly come across this:

The man who more than anyone brought about the solution of the teenage problem was Eric Ridley [a lightly disguised Eric Liddell]. It is rare indeed that a person has the good fortune to meet a saint, but he came as close to it as anyone I have ever known. Often in an evening of that last year, I (headed for some pleasant rendezvous with my girlfriend) would pass the games room and peer in to see what the missionaries had going for the teenagers. As often as not, Eric would be bent over a chessboard or a model boat, or directing some sort of square dance – absorbed, weary and interested, pouring all of himself into this effort to capture the minds and imaginations of those penned-up youths. If anyone could have done it, he could. A track man, he had won the 400 metres in the twenties for England [Scotland, actually], and then had come to China as a missionary. In camp he was in his middle forties, lithe and springy of step and, above all, overflowing with good humour and love of life. He was aided by others, to be sure. But it was Eric's enthusiasm and charm that carried the day with the whole effort.

This is an astonishing tribute from the acerbic Mr Gilkey. Eric, we discover, was distinctively different in every area where his fellow-missionaries – or some, at any rate – were at their least attractive. He bridged the gulf between the missionaries and the businessmen, and was respected by both. In the Great Cigarette Crisis, he had stood by his principles and destroyed the cigarettes he could otherwise have sold. He prayed privately and quietly. He lived out his morality, thrusting it on nobody. His smile was infectious.

Eric Liddell, of course, was already a celebrity by the time he arrived at the camp. 'Don't stare now,' one internee had whispered to a new arrival as they trudged through the camp, 'but that man coming towards us is Eric Liddell.' The newcomer remembered the occasion for a long time: 'I was too limp to connect the oncoming stranger with the well-known Olympic athlete of some years before, but I glanced aside to note the man on the path. He was not very tall, rather thin, very bronzed with sun and air. He was wearing the most comical shirt I had ever seen, though I was to get accustomed to similar garments in that place. It was made, I learned later, from a pair of Mrs Liddell's curtains.'

If there was one satisfaction that Eric was discovering in Weihsien camp, it was being able to indulge his passion for excessively colourful garments without anyone disapproving of them. Florence's curtains were nothing special among an exotic array of clothing that comprised everything from school uniforms to tattered fur coats. One lady who arrived at the camp took one look at the crowd of people at the gate and thought they were insane. They were bleary-eyed and haggard, and their clothes were a pathetic echo of the different life-styles from which they had been snatched.

When Eric had first arrived in the camp he had immediately been assigned to the school as a maths and science teacher. He was also put in charge of camp sports, which involved not only whipping up enthusiasm and rounding people up for teams, but looking after all the equipment. He would tear up curtains, sheets and tablecloths of his own to mend hockey-sticks in winter and sew up baseballs in summer.

He also acted as warden of Blocks 23 and 24, two large buildings housing 230 unattached men and women, boys and girls. It was his job to collect supplies and make sure all his charges were in place at the roll-call every morning and evening. With those in the room he had to share such daily duties as fetching water, dumping dirty water and rubbish and cleaning the room. In the evenings he tutored youngsters who wanted to keep up their studies in camp. He was also put in charge of the Weihsien Christian Fellowship. Yet another of his jobs was that of chief translator for the Japanese in the camp. These were his official tasks. But you would also see him around the camp mending a hockey-stick here, carrying coal for an old person there; bent over some game to keep a youngster amused, helping a child with her books. 'Really he was without a doubt the person most in demand and most respected and loved in camp,' said one former internee. 'One night he was telling us at our place how many hours he figured he did a week, and I was amazed that anyone could carry such a timetable.'

The games that Langdon Gilkey had seen him organizing included chess and draughts tournaments, craft shows, dart contests, one-act plays and home-made puppet shows. The trouble with the teenagers never recurred after this programme was arranged for them. It ought to be mentioned that Eric was not alone in his work with these young children. It was teachers like him, from among the much-maligned missionaries, who devised the programme of games and entertainments while the the parents did nothing. It was they who gave up their free time to keep the youngsters amused. The missionaries were also among the group who eventually solved the toilet problem. Then a few Catholic priests and nuns, aided by some of the Protestant missionaries, tied cloths round their faces, borrowed boots and mops, and tackled the horrendous job of unstopping the toilets. In the end, they prevented a recurrence of the problem by suggesting that the inmates should flush the toilets after each use with a half-bucket of water.

The missionaries, for all the criticisms he had of some of them, win a rare tribute from Gilkey in the end. He writes:

There was a quality seemingly unique to the missionary group, namely, naturally and without pretence to respond to a need which everyone else recognized only to turn aside. Much of this went unnoticed, but our camp could scarcely have survived as well as it did without it. If there were any evidences of the grace of God observable on the surface of our camp existence, they were to be found here.

The many former internees who remember Eric Liddell at that camp offer vivid, affectionate accounts of the things they used to find him doing.

Eric taught when he could [wrote one]. He coached boys and girls hoping to specialize in university when the time for release came. For one girl alone he made a beautiful notebook full of drawings of apparatus which she ought to have been using, but could not, and with that to guide her she did learn enough later to enter Melbourne University straight from the camp when the war was over.

Besides this work, he organized all the games. Evening after evening he tore up, with a grim smile, all of the sheets his wife had left for his use, just to bind up the injured blades of the few precious hockey-sticks which had somehow made their way into internment with us. He gummed the strips of linen with Chinese glue melted down over a one-candle-power peanut-oil lamp. He took over the 'prepites' of Chefoo school . . . so that their weary teacher could put her feet up for a few precious minutes once a week.

It was fun to see him teaching them rounders! He arranged for the Americans to run a series of baseball matches, though he took no responsibility for any Sunday games, which they asked for . . . To encourage the eighteen-year-old lads to keep fit, he would run the circumference of the camp within the walls and teach them something of running techniques.

This was not all his work by any means. He was on the Camp Discipline Committee, a most important organization of our own which prevented many a silly scrape from getting to the ears of the Japanese guards. He also taught Bible Class on Sundays. Most of all he was the man we turned to when personal relationships got just too impossible. We lived in large dormitories with but six feet by three feet of space for ourselves and what belongings we had. He had a gentle, humorous way of soothing ruffled tempers and bringing to one's mind some bygone happiness or the prospect of some future interest round the corner 'when we got out'.

In a camp rife with criticism and back-biting and gossip, there was no one who had a bad word to say of Eric Liddell. His attitude to everyone was the same. You would find him talking to the businessman just the same way as to the Roman Catholic priest or the child from Chefoo. There is something immensely touching about the tributes to his life from this period, something about the kind of details they all remember, that leaps out with the force of truth. For instance, there is the story of how he had his Edinburgh presentation gold watch carefully weighed and valued, because there was a shortage of softball gear and money was needed to buy more. The sacrifice was not required in the end, because money came in at the last minute. But the gesture was noticed.

It is fascinating to talk to people who were youngsters at the time, and listen to them thinking aloud about the man whom every child in the camp knew; people like Mrs Isabel Herron, for instance, who, as a fourteen-year-old called Isabel Harris, came to Weihsien from Chefoo school. She now lives in Edinburgh, and still remembers Eric Liddell:

'My memory of Eric is at the side of the hockey field, examining all our sticks as we came off. We didn't have a chance of replacing a stick then; it had to go on being mended and mended. And I remember Eric taking the sticks away and meticulously binding them up and always having them ready for the next game. He never seemed to be too busy. He was always around helping us . . .

'I remember him being angry on the hockey pitch with someone for playing foul or something. If you felt you had done something wrong then you would probably hear from him . . .

'He was a friend; someone around if you needed him. He used

to spend a lot of time carrying water for infirm people and carrying coal . . .

'He wasn't a very good preacher, but he certainly had us all there listening to him just because his personality or his sincerity or whatever it was came across so strongly . . .

'When Eric died, one of the women in the camp, a Russian prostitute, told my mother that Eric Liddell was the only man who had ever done anything for her, and not wanted to be repaid in kind. I think that when she first moved into camp he'd gone and put some shelves up for her. She was a woman living on her own, she didn't have anyone to do that kind of thing. And it didn't matter what walk of life a person came from, Eric wouldn't judge anybody . . . There *were* missionaries in the camp who wouldn't have helped someone like her. But Eric didn't see things that way . . .

'He would do anything rather than talk about his Olympic feat: not through false modesty, but he was too interested in the present. He wasn't particularly interested in the past. It was one very important part of his life, but I think there were also some equally important parts of his life . . .

'It's hard to explain . . . but missionaries can be people who keep themselves so much apart. There were some people who were more interested in, how shall I say, their own kind, and not so interested in the others. And missionaries who didn't really have time for these other people's children, and just worked with the missionaries' children. But Eric worked right across the board with everyone. It keeps on coming across in my memory of him. He must have been very strong, because he really did treat us all the same.'

Another Chefoo child, Norman Cliff, wrote a book of his camp experiences, called *Courtyard of the Happy Way*. There he calls Eric Liddell, 'the most outstanding Weihsien personality . . . in his early forties, quiet-spoken and with a permanent smile. Eric was the finest Christian man I have ever had the privilege of meeting.'

What they keep coming back to again and again, these people, is the way he *lived* his Christianity. Eric is portrayed as the Christ-figure here at the camp just as much as he was among the Chinese in Siaochang. He befriends the prostitute and the despised businessman; he carries coal for the weak and teaches the young; he gets ready to sell his gold watch and tears up his sheets for hockey-sticks. And yet he is still the same Eric, marching around in a multi-coloured shirt made out of old curtains and looking extremely ordinary and nothing special at all.

One of the hardest decisions he had to make in the camp was what to do about Sunday games. No, he said, there were to be no games on Sunday; it was a principle from which he had never deviated. But many of the teenagers protested against this and decided to organize a hockey game by themselves despite him – boys against girls. It ended in a free fight, because there was no referee. On the following Sunday, Eric turned out on that field to act as referee. It is a most illuminating detail of his life: he would not run on a Sunday for an Olympic gold medal in the 100 metres and all the glory in the world; but he refereed a game on a Sunday, he broke his unbreakable principle, just to keep a handful of imprisoned youngsters at peace with each other. It speaks volumes about the man.

From time to time Eric preached at church services in the camp, and his subject was invariably the Sermon on the Mount, or St Paul's hymn of love in 1 Corinthians. 'Though I speak with the tongues of men and of angels and have not love,' he would tell his listeners, 'I am become as sounding brass or a tinkling cymbal.' These words of St Paul were the cornerstone of his faith, these and Christ's Sermon on the Mount – blessed are the poor in spirit, the mourners, the meek, the merciful, the pure in heart, the peacemakers, the persecuted. This was the way he believed love could be translated into living.

He had once written a little booklet called *The Sermon on the Mount: For Sunday School Teachers*. It was published as he left Tientsin to begin his work out in the country in 1937. In it he had encapsulated his years of study and insight.

'Blessed are the *meek*: for they shall inherit the earth, [he notes there], St Matthew 5:5 (see Psalm 37,11). *Meek* – Gentle of temper, humble, kind, mild, yielding, unassuming. Note Aristotle's account of it as the character of one who has the passion of resentment under control, and who is therefore tranquil and untroubled. Control because of clear conscience. Meekness and weakness often associated together. What is the difference? Both may be kind and gentle. Is the difference the element of fear?

Meek – kind and gentle and fearless.
Weak – kind and gentle and led by fear.
Meek – is love in the presence of wrong.

In another book, published in 1942, his last full year before internment, called *Prayers for Daily Use*, he wrote about obedience as the key to knowing God: 'OBEDIENCE to God's will is the secret of spiritual knowledge and insight. It is not willingness to know, but willingness to DO (obey) God's Will that brings certainty.'

These were the things he talked about in the camp, in big church services and small meditation groups alike. It was always the same – always love and obedience and the fragrance of a God-enfolded life. And, as always, people listened to him less for his oratory than for that something else they could never define – '. . . his personality or his sincerity or whatever it was', as Isabel Herron tried rather helplessly to express it. What was his secret? People were asking it then as some are still asking it today. Another internee came up with her own answer:

'What was his secret? Once I asked him, but I really knew already, for my husband was in his dormitory and shared the secret with him. Every morning about 6 a.m., with curtains tightly drawn to keep in the shining of our peanut-oil lamp, lest the prowling sentries would think someone was trying to escape, he used to climb out of his top bunk, past the sleeping forms of his dormitory mates. Then, at the small Chinese table, the two men would sit close together with the light just enough to illumine their Bibles and notebooks. Silently they read, prayed, thought about the day's duties, noted what should be done. Eric was a man of prayer not only at set times – though he did not like to miss a prayer meeting or communion service when such could be arranged. He talked to God all the time, naturally, as one can who enters the "school of prayer" to learn this way of inner discipline. He seemed to have no weighty mental problems: his life was grounded in God, in faith, and in trust.'

But the strains of camp life were gradually taking their toll of

165

the internees, particularly those over forty. There were mental breakdowns and cases of typhoid, malaria, dysentery. The heat could be unbearable and, worst of all, supplies of food grew more and more meagre as 1944 drew to an end. Eric, too, was feeling the strain.

When Annie Buchan arrived at Weihsien internment camp several months after Eric, she noticed a difference in his appearance. 'What's happened to Eric? ... He's slowed down ... He's walking slowly, he's talking slowly,' she went round saying to people. No one else in the camp really noticed any change in Eric; it took the eye of someone who had known him for years but had not seen him for a long time to realize that Eric had lost something of his bounce and spring.

The former matron of the Siaochang Hospital had originally thought she was going to escape internment. She had been given a card from the authorities saying that, because she had been 'humane', she would be exempt. But one day, Japanese guards came and told her she must leave the British Consulate in Peking, where she had been nursing an invalid friend until the lady's death. She was to go to Weihsien as an act of reprisal: two men had escaped from the camp, and she was to be interned in their place.

She found that Eric, whom she had not seen for some years, was doing far too much work. 'Eric had a very heavy responsibility,' she says, 'more than he should have had, I think. But people depended on him so much. He was teaching science to the children from Chefoo, and that was enough for him alone. But he was so willing that he was doing a lot of odd jobs for people. They depended on him to organize all the camp entertainments. There were other teachers there who could have done it, but Eric was always there. It was too much.'

By the autumn of 1944, Eric was losing some of his resilience: he was also feeling the strain of being separated for so long from his family. Some of the internees were surprised to discover later that he had a wife and family at all, because he so rarely complained of missing them. 'There were other people in the same position,' says Isabel Herron, 'who went round moaning that they had not seen their wives. But Eric was so busy cheering other people up that he kept his own miseries and problems very

166

much to himself . . . He was a very private person. I remember being quite surprised at finding out how close he and Flo actually were.'

By this time, after eighteen months of internment, even Eric's phenomenal energy had been sapped by privation and hunger. The constant games-playing for the benefit of the youngsters was taking its toll. The inhabitants of Weihsien internment camp, without knowing it, were slowly starving. Had it not been for the arrival of Red Cross parcels at the end of January 1945, they would all have been in desperate trouble.

Eric, of course, never complained about the conditions, or his health. But he made no attempt to hide his private feelings from Annie Buchan, who knew him so well. Whenever the pair had any spare time, they would go and sit in the open courtyard and out would come Eric's snapshots of Florence and the children. Poring over the photographs, Eric would give her any news he had had from Canada – which was usually very little, because letters were taking months to arrive. In one of these quiet talks he told her something she has never forgotten: 'My big worry, Annie,' he said, 'is that I didn't give Flo enough of my time.' He also said to her once that he could not see any future – everything seemed blank. 'And that wasn't like Eric,' says Annie. 'He had always been full of hope.'

In the middle of January 1945, Eric, who was suffering already from incipient malnutrition like everyone else in the camp, had an attack of what was thought to be influenza with severe sinusitis; but the serious inflammation did not respond to treatment as readily as it should have done. He suffered from agonizing headaches, and would lie in his room with his eyes bandaged, wanting nothing but quiet.

As soon as Annie Buchan heard that he was ill she marched straight to the men's dormitory to see him in defiance of the camp rules. 'As soon as I had seen him I went straight to the head doctor at the camp, and said Eric must be brought to hospital. He said there was no room. I said I thought Eric must have hospital treatment. So he was brought in. But he was so courageous, he would never say what he felt was wrong with him; so they just said, "Oh, he'll get over it." '

In hospital he had what was thought to be partial stroke.

While he was recovering from that, the few visitors he was allowed reported that he seemed bright but occasionally 'wandered', and sounded distressed about his family in Canada. He had a strange look in one eye, and he spoke haltingly; he had difficulty in walking, for his right leg was partially paralysed. But he remained cheerful, and people who went to see him came away cheered in turn. With one young couple he knew, he discussed their approaching marriage; he also discussed the bridesmaid's dress, despite the exigencies of the camp wardrobe.

The doctors were worried about him, and suspected a brain tumour. They held long and earnest consultations about him, but with the equipment at their disposal in the camp there was little they could do. Apart from anything else, he was suffering from both nervous and physical exhaustion; a period of complete rest was prescribed.

For a time he seemed to rally, and started moving about again. He was still getting these piercing pains in his head, however. When a solicitous friend asked if his head were any better, he replied, 'To answer that question I'd need to know what is going on inside my head.' He told a veteran missionary colleague from Siaochang, Mr C. H. B. Longman, that the doctor thought he had had a nervous breakdown. The pain in his head had been causing him bouts of depression for some time; but what concerned him more was that he felt it was a sign of spiritual weakness in himself that he could not bear everything as cheerfully as he would have liked, in faith. 'There is just one thing that troubles me,' he told a fellow missionary in his slow, limping speech. 'I ought to have been able to cast it all on the Lord, and not to have broken under it.'

For a while, however, he seemed to be on the mend. He was allowed out to have tea with his friends. He even insisted on climbing four flights of stairs to visit his colleague in his room in the top storey of the hospital block. 'It was like reaching for the stars,' said the nurse who helped him; but he made it.

On the last day of his life he went out for a stroll in the afternoon, and met the wife of one of his Tientsin colleagues. They walked for about fifteen minutes. He seemed his usual cheerful self again.

'Have you heard from Flo?' she asked him.

Yes, he'd had one of her letters, he said. He seemed tired, and spoke haltingly.

'You ought to be resting more,' she said.

'No, I must get my walking legs again,' he replied.

Eric must have been on his way to the post office to post his last letter to his wife. It was dated the same day, 21 February 1945. The Japanese allowed the internees only 100 words per letter, so they had to write in a kind of telegraphese. Florence only received it several months later:

Was carrying too much responsibility. Slight nervous breakdown. Am much better after month in hospital. Doctor suggests changing my work. Giving up teaching and taking up physical work like baking . . . A good change. Keep me in touch with the news. Enjoying comfort and parcels. Special love to you and the children. – Eric.

That same evening, after he had written this letter, he had a spasm of choking and coughing. One of his old Sunday school pupils at Tientsin was with him at the time, and he clutched her arm as the pain seized him. Then the spasm passed, and later in the evening he was laughing and joking again with one of the missionaries' children. Suddenly he took another attack. The little girl who was with him ran out and called for the doctor, who had him moved to a separate and single room.

There, Annie Buchan, who had just come off nursing duty, came to his bedside:

'I asked him how he was feeling, and he said no one had a clue what was wrong. That was the phrase he used – "They haven't a clue." After that I simply refused to leave. I stayed. One or two of the doctors were standing in the middle of the ward next door, and talking about Eric, and I just went in to them and said, "Do you realize Eric is dying?" Somebody said, "Nonsense." I went back into Eric's room, and by this time Eric was pretty far through. And he just said to me, "Annie, it's complete surrender." Then he took a convulsion and vomited all over me, and then he was gone into a coma and he never recovered.

' "Surrender"? Yes, that's what he said. I was holding him. I could hardly hear him. He started saying it. He could hardly get the words out, but he definitely said "complete surrender".'

Surrender. A strange word for a hero to utter with his dying breath, especially a man who had never given up, ever, particularly when the challenge was greatest. It is only really meaningful in the context of the faith by which he had lived, and by which he was now completely surrendering himself to his God.

Next day an autopsy revealed an inoperable tumour on the left side of his brain. It was this that had caused the agony of the preceding weeks, and the massive haemorrhage that eventually killed him.

11

'There's No Way Anyone Like Him Could Die'

On 2 May 1945, more than two months after Eric's death, two family friends arrived at the house where Florence Liddell was staying in Toronto, her parents' home. They asked if her mother were in.

'I invited them in and I sensed there was something wrong. So finally I said to them, "Have you got bad news? Is it one of the boys?" (I had two brothers, you know.) Even then it never crossed my mind that it would be Eric.

'About a month before this visit, I had had the strangest feeling. I was standing at the stove and I thought, "If you turn round, Eric is standing there." I could just feel vibrations. He was so full of life and bouncy. And he said, "It's OK, Flossie. Everything is going to be all right." (Flossie is the name he always used to tease me; it used to make me mad!) I thought my nerves were going. For three weeks I was conscious of his presence in this way. But it never crossed my mind that he had died. I am sure that somehow or other he was allowed to come back.

'I was terribly crushed when I got the news. I was all for jumping off the bridge. But again his influence was just *there*; as if he were saying, "Florence, what are you going to accomplish by jumping off the bridge?" I was thinking I would catch up with Eric that way, but he would just look at me as if to say,

171

"Flo, what about the three little girls I've left in your care?"
And that stopped me.

'I had had no hint that he was even ill. Three or four Red Cross letters from him came after I heard he was dead, and one mentioned that he was in hospital and that they thought he might be working too hard. He got these terrible headaches at that time and he got depressed because he had always thought his faith would carry him through. A couple from the Salvation Army wrote to me afterwards and said they had seen him putting his hand to the wall to steady himself sometimes. That's when I really felt bad.

'He had told me nothing about what life was like in the camp. He just talked about the children and said he was helping with the sports. They had to be very circumspect in their letters. Generally, on the back of the letter form there was a space where you could reply; and it would take from six months to a year for a letter to go back and forwards.

'Eric was ten years older than me, you know. I'd like to have seen what he looked like today. He was eternally young – even though he had very little hair. He used to make jokes about it, but his mother was very perturbed and swore it was because he took too many showers.

'I liked the way they portrayed him in the film – *Chariots of Fire*, is that its name? It was just exactly Eric. It moved me very much. I especially liked the way they had him in Paris telling the Prince of Wales he would not run on a Sunday. The way he was so quiet but stood up for himself and firmly answered back.

'He certainly threw himself into his running, didn't he? The way he threw his head back – it was so ridiculous! Boy, I couldn't understand how he could even see. When I ever asked him he just said, "I knew where I was going all right." He had the most beautiful laugh.'

Five years after Eric's death, Florence remarried. Their eldest daughter Tricia was sixteen by then. Florence's second husband was a cousin, a Canadian cattle-farmer called Murray Hall, with whom she had a long and happy marriage until his death in the 1960s. She inherited three step-children, and together they had a seventh child – another daughter for Florence, called Jeannie.

172

By 1981, Eric would have had nine grandchildren. Patricia, Heather and Maureen, remedying his own propensity to produce females, had produced seven boys and two girls among them. The children all knew about their grandfather and were tickled pink about a film being made about him. 'And is it *really* my grandfather?' one diminutive fellow was heard to ask wonderingly.

Florence's two husbands were very different kinds of men. Her second husband was a more rough-and-ready sort of man than Eric: 'But we had a very good marriage. I said when Eric died that I would never marry again for security, only for love – and I never thought that would happen. But I found it was possible to love like that again.

'But Eric? I consider myself privileged to have been married to him. We were only married eleven years, and for four of these we were separated. But I learned so much from him. It was a super marriage.'

Weihsien internment camp, on the snowy February day after Eric died, was cold and numb with shock. Hardly anyone had known he was ill, and the end had come very swiftly.

'I can just remember the shock going through the camp,' says Isabel Herron. 'It can't be true, we were saying . . . there's no way that anyone like him could die.'

Langdon Gilkey reports: 'The entire camp, especially its youth, was stunned for days, so great was the vacuum that Eric's death had left.'

On Saturday, 24 February, they held his funeral. It was a bleak windswept day. People from all over the camp crowded into the hall for the service, and those who couldn't get in stood outside. The numbers waiting in the cold outside the hall were an unprecedented tribute. For the first time, missionaries and city businessmen mingled in fellowship, their presence together an unspoken testimony to the man. There must have been at least one person from most of the twenty-one nationalities in the camp. People who would never have been expected to attend were there – people one would think had nothing in common with the things he stood for. And many were in tears.

Those inside waited in silence while the music of 'I Know that My Redeemer Liveth' on the piano sounded round the hall. The table was piled high with wreaths: from missionary colleagues; from the men in his dormitory and the people he had supervised as warden; from the Boy Scouts and Girl Guides whom he had helped keep going as an organization in the camp; from the children of the Weihsien School; from the officers of the Salvation Army; from everybody.

One of the senior missionaries, the Rev. Arnold Bryson, gave a short address, the first of a long, long stream of tributes to Eric Liddell in the months to come that would have made him shrivel with embarrassment.

'Although his activities lay chiefly in the religious, athletic and educational departments of camp life, his genial, winsome disposition and his readiness to help anyone in need attracted both young and old. From his humble and modest demeanour no one could have guessed that here was a man with an international reputation on the running track and football field.

'The sudden removal of such a man in the prime of his life, and at the peak of his powers, inevitably raises questions in our hearts. Why did God take him from a world in which such men are so sorely needed today? But God makes no mistakes. His thoughts are not our thoughts, neither are His ways our ways. Perhaps in God's loving purpose, by Eric's early promotion to higher service he was spared years of acute suffering, and we can only bow to God's will.

'Yesterday a man said to me, "Of all the men I have known, Eric Liddell was the one in whose character and life the spirit of Jesus Christ was pre-eminently manifested." And all of us who were privileged to know him with any intimacy echo this judgement. What was the secret of his consecrated life and far-reaching influence? Absolute surrender to God's will as revealed in Jesus Christ. His was a God-controlled life and he followed his Master and Lord with a devotion that never flagged and with an intensity of purpose that made men see both the reality and power of true religion.'

A prayer, a hymn, the Lord's Prayer, the Benediction and a closing voluntary, 'O Rest in the Lord' – and the funeral service was over. Then the coffin was borne by his friends through a

174

guard of honour, composed of the children from the Chefoo and the Weihsien schools, to the quiet cemetery in the Japanese officers' headquarters, where several other internees were buried. There, at the windy graveside, the huge company repeated the Beatitudes from the Sermon on the Mount that had been Eric Liddell's special inspiration. 'Blessed are the meek; for they shall inherit the earth,' they chorused, as the wind lifted their hair and tugged at their coats. 'Blessed are the pure in heart; for they shall see God. Blessed are the peacemakers; for they shall be called the children of God . . .' Then his body was lowered into the grave, and the people began to disperse.

Ten days later, the big Edwardian-style church at the camp was filled to overflowing for a memorial service conducted by Eric's old friend, schoolmaster, colleague and flat-mate, the Rev. A. P. Cullen. They all sang the hymn, 'Be Still, My Soul'. It had always been Eric's favourite. Twenty years earlier, he had written to Florence in Canada while they were still engaged: 'I often play it over. It goes to the beautiful tune, *Finlandia* – a calm, restful, beautiful tune . . .' On the afternoon of his death, he had scrawled a few things on some scraps of paper; among them were the first line and a broken phrase or two of that hymn: 'Be still, my soul.' The congregation stayed in their seats, and sang Eric's hymn very quietly and softly. There are people all over the world who still think instantly of Eric Liddell whenever they hear the strains of that hymn, and are carried back to a church in an internment camp in China all these years ago.

'I always associate him with "Be still, my soul; the Lord is on thy side",' says a former Chefoo schoolgirl. 'I think it's because I remember him as such a still, serene person. I felt things were going to turn out all right in the end, when I heard that hymn at the service that day.'

Eric had once told Florence that he would come back and haunt her if she ever allowed at his funeral any of the eulogies that always made him so uncomfortable. Maybe he did just that. But he would have run a mile if he could have heard the eulogies that flowed from the church in Weihsien that day.

'I have known Eric for thirty-three years,' the Rev. A. P. Cullen told the huge gathering, 'since he was a schoolboy of ten at Eltham College. I have been in frequent contact with him for the last twenty years. After his family left for Canada, he and I lived together, just the two of us, in my flat till January 1942. From then until he came here fourteen months later, almost every day I went for a long walk with him. And from my knowledge of him, gained in this close association over many years, I say that Eric is the most remarkable example in my experience of a man of average ability and talents developing those talents to an amazing degree, and even appearing to acquire new talents from time to time, through the power of the Holy Spirit. He was, literally, God-controlled, in his thought, judgement, actions, words, to an extent I have never seen surpassed, and rarely seen equalled.'

He described the regular and rapid progress of Eric's spiritual development as being 'as phenomenal as the speed with which, in a 100 yards race, after being yards behind at half-way, he would catch up and pass the winning-post an easy first, leaving the other competitors standing . . . Indeed, the growth of his spiritual life affords a remarkable parallel to his methods of running a race, for one of the astonishing things in his victories on the track . . . was that he was always a bit slow in getting off the mark, mainly, I am convinced, because his fine conscience would never allow him to "beat the gun".'

Then he spoke about the word which had been Eric's last – *surrender*: 'Let us now turn to the way in which he tried to work out that ideal. First of all, absolute surrender to the will of God. Absolute surrender – those words were often on his lips, the conception was always in his mind; that God should have absolute control over every part of his life. It was towards the attainment of that ideal that he directed all his mental and spiritual energies.'

W. E. McLaren, a shipping agent in Tientsin, who had played threequarter beside Eric as a rugby international for Scotland, spoke of Liddell the sportsman: 'Many a time he was lain for by his opponents, whose tactics were at least doubtful, but never would he repay them in their own coin. His method was invariable – he merely played better rugby and made them look like second-raters.'

But perhaps the most remarkable tribute was one that was not made in public, but in private. It was confided to a day-to-day diary that was kept throughout the vicissitudes and sorrows of those months in captivity:

> February 24. Eric's funeral today.
> He was not particularly clever, and not conspicuously able, but he was good.
> He was naturally reserved and tended to live in a world of his own, but he gave of himself unstintedly.
> He always shrank from revealing his deepest needs and distresses, so that while he bore the burdens of many, very few could help to bear his.
> His fame as an athlete helped him a good deal. He certainly didn't look like a great runner, but the fact that he had been one gave him a self-confidence that men of his type don't have.
> He wasn't a great leader, or an inspired thinker, but he knew what he ought to do, and he did it.
> He was a true disciple of the Master and worthy of the highest places amongst the saints . . .

Was Eric Liddell a saint, then? Or a hero? Or just someone who had caught the public imagination, a famous name, a superstar of his time? It is difficult to know just how the man in the street regarded him, but there is no doubt that the news of his death was received in Scotland with a feeling of shock and a universal sense of loss. It was felt not just in the religious, and the rugby and university circles to which Eric had belonged, but on the football terracings, in the cinema queues, and on the street corners, where once again his name was on the billboards.

'Scotland has lost a son who did her proud every hour of his life,' wrote the Glasgow *Evening News*.

'One of the best known and most admired men who ever took part in sport, whose devotion to his principles won him the highest esteem.' That was the Edinburgh *Evening News*. In another article, a leading sports writer summed him up as 'Probably the most illustrious type of muscular Christianity ever known.' The newspapers were never short of a phrase, or a headline, where Liddell was concerned.

Memorial services were held in many parts of Scotland, and in many countries, including Canada. In Glasgow, people packed into Dundas Street Congregational Church, where Eric's father had been ordained before leaving for China all those years before. All the leading churchmen were there, the heads of missionary societies, missionaries, students, sportsmen, D. P. Thomson, Eric's brother Rob (now home from China), his younger brother Ernest and his sister, Mrs Jenny Somerville. There was the manager of Rangers Football Club, the legendary Bill Struth, who could always count on an extra 10,000 at the 'gate' at the annual Rangers Sports Meeting when Eric Liddell was running; Duncan (Dunky) Wright, the British marathon champion; John M. Bannerman, the immortal Scottish rugby internationalist and champion of Gaeldom.

Alan Morton, one of Scotland's greatest footballers and darling of the terracings, read the lesson, and one by one the tributes were paid:

BILL STRUTH: 'He deliberately sacrificed a fine chance of one Olympic title because of his religious convictions. He just as certainly put aside a career of brilliance and affluence to serve his master in the most practical of all forms of Christianity. In his work in China he created an opportunity for the talents with which he was so richly endowed; courage, determination, skill, endurance, and self-sacrifice, to be utilized to the full. Sport gave to Eric Liddell its highest honours; nevertheless, it is true to say that he honoured sport rather than sport honouring him.

'The details of the last few years of his life are not yet known to us, but we can be certain that under the most severe of all trials, he exhibited just those qualities which he showed in his sporting life. His life was perhaps a short one; but his work, as he clearly saw it, and, as we believe, divinely inspired, carried out away from the applause of the crowd, will remain a source of inspiration to many.

'In these days of exaggerated hero-worship and publicity for sports champions, Eric Liddell's example reminds us to put things in their proper perspective. Sport to him was sport – not the be-all and end-all – and success in it did not prevent him from picking out the things spiritual from the things temporal. His was an example which must have helped others to make a similar choice.'

DUNKY WRIGHT, Scotland's greatest long-distance runner: 'Eric was greater than an athlete; he was a Crusade. He was without doubt the most glorious runner I have ever seen. Never has there been a greater need for a man with such a high moral and virile Christian character like Eric Liddell to be set as an example to our young people. I would suggest that a picture of Eric Liddell be hung in every youth club and sports pavilion in our country, with the title, "Eric Liddell: a Christian sportsman!" '

THE REV. ROBERT DOBBIE, who had been one of the founders of the Scottish Student Campaign Movement in 1922: 'He was "a very parfit gentil knight".'

In Edinburgh, the service was in Morningside Congregational Church, of which Eric had been a member in his student days. There were nearly 1,000 people present, including Eric's sister and two brothers. Among the speakers was Mr George Robertson, Eric's old headmaster at Eltham College and now Headmaster of George Watson's College, Edinburgh. Dunky Wright spoke again, as did D. P. Thomson.

In Toronto's Carlton Street United Church, the Rev. T. T. Faichney, a Perthshire man who had been minister of the Union Church in Tientsin, told the gathering, which no doubt included Florence and the girls, 'Everything that Eric did, he did well; he had a passion for perfection. For one who was among the world's fleetest of foot, I often marvelled that he was so slow in speech and in the things he did. But it was because nothing less than the best was good enough.'

He held up a copy of *The Sermon on the Mount* – the collection of Sunday school lessons that Eric had published for the teachers of the Tientsin church when he was the Sunday school superintendent there: 'It is the best thing that I have on the Sermon on the Mount in my library. Going through it one marvels at his erudition, his wide reading and his spiritual perception.'

A big National Committee was formed to launch the Eric Liddell Memorial Fund, with Sir Iain Colquhoun of Luss as chairman, and all the great names in church and business, the universities and sport, on the committee. Fund-raising functions were held in towns and villages, church halls and town halls. Collections were taken at football matches, rugby grounds, sports meetings, fêtes and charity balls. Business firms donated advertising space and money poured in from private contributions. Very soon there was enough in the fund to educate Eric's three daughters and found the Eric Liddell Challenge Trophy for the best performance of the year in the Scottish Schools Athletic Association Championship meeting.

Dunky Wright used to coach boys for the championships, and he never failed to remind them of Eric's gold medal and how he came to win the 400 metres instead of the 100 metres. 'Now,' he would tell them, 'to win an Olympic event is a great honour, perhaps the greatest athletic honour. But Eric Liddell is not remembered for this achievement, but as the man who wouldn't run on a Sunday.'

An Eric Liddell Memorial Room was opened in the St Ninian's Conference and Training Centre in Edinburgh. Eltham College built a new boarding house and named it after him. The 3rd Hong Kong Sea Scout Group was just one of many Scout patrols to establish a Liddell Patrol. The Perthshire town of Crieff claimed to have the only Eric Liddell Boys' Club in the world, and eighteen months after his death there was a memorial service held by rugby enthusiasts in the Borders. There were thirteen Scottish Internationalists in St Paul's Parish Church, Galashiels, and D. P. Thomson told them: 'It's nearly twenty-one years since Liddell's athletic career in this country closed, and nearly a year and a half since he died. For what other athlete could such a gathering be assembled, in a town in which he has never lived, and a district to which he only paid one or two visits?'

In *Rugger My Pleasure*, the sports writer A. A. Thomson summed up what the sporting world thought of Eric Liddell:

During the worst period of his imprisonment he was, through his courage and cheerfulness, a tower of strength and sanity to his fellow prisoners. To many sufferers he brought the only comfort that captivity allowed. It is one of the deep sadnesses of life, that while so many survived the years of captivity, E. H. Liddell, who had helped so many, did not. He was one of the most chivalrous of Scots, as an athlete and as a man.

Since the Second World War, Eric Liddell has been the

subject of magazine and newspaper articles, and radio and television programmes. Sunday school courses have been based on his life, church congregations have listened to sermons about him. Even an Eric Liddell strip cartoon found its way into the pages of a boys' comic.

And now there is an Eric Liddell film.

12

'The Emotion
Comes from Within'

The 1980s, you would think, are hardly the most auspicious time
for a film about a man whose life could have come straight from
the pages of the *Boys' Own* paper. Ours is a generation which is
not supposed to like straightforward, clean-cut heroes like Eric
Liddell. The heroes of the 1960s and 1970s were the seekers who
never find, the nihilists, the rebels, the intellectuals racked by
doubt, the Eastern mystics who sought their serenity in re-
nouncing the world. Now the inheritors of that legacy, the
generation of the 1980s, are being asked to respond to a man
whose life was the very opposite of that: a man who prayed
every morning and refused to run on a Sunday; a man untroubled
by doubts, who found his serenity in total immersion in the
world; a man who had the kingdom of sport at his feet and
renounced it for the obscurity of a perilous career as a missionary
in China.

David Puttnam, who produced *Chariots of Fire*, knows it is
not an 'expedient' film to make. But he revels in the sheer
inexpediency of it. It has been a catharsis, a purging of himself
and his career.

The idea for the film came in 1977 when he was lying ill in a
rented house in Los Angeles, having produced *Midnight Express*.
He picked up a book casually from the library to while away the
time; it was *The Official History of the Olympic Games* by Bill

Henry. And in it he found something that seized his attention. In the chapter on the 1924 Olympics in Paris he read this:

Undoubtedly the dark-horse honours of the 1924 games went to E. H. Liddell, a bandy-legged little Scottish divinity student who, driven from his favourite event, the 100 metres, by his religious scruples, which prevented him from running on Sunday, surprised himself and everybody else by winning the 400 metres in record time.

Liddell, an awkward runner who obviously was unfamiliar with the distance, set out like a scared jackrabbit at the sound of the gun and fought off the challenge of H. M. Fitch of the United States down the stretch to cover the distance in 47 3/5 seconds. Not satisfied with this performance, he was a good third in the 200 metres, which was won by Jackson Scholz of the United States.

As Puttnam was to discover from subsequent research, this account of Liddell's exploits at the Paris Olympics was not entirely accurate (Liddell was a science student at the time, for instance, and the 200 metres came *before* the 400 metres); but by now Puttnam's imagination had been well and truly fired.

'I am always reading that kind of book,' he says, 'and I couldn't understand why I hadn't come across this tale before. It read for me like a wonderful *Boys' Own* story. I wanted to find out more.'

As he read more about the Paris Olympics, he also developed an interest in the figure of Harold Abrahams, the Jewish student who had won the 100 metres gold medal after Eric Liddell declined to take part. With that, the idea for a film began to take shape. The dramatic potential in the complementary lives of the two men began to excite him more and more. They were so different, Liddell and Abrahams – different in background, in temperament, in religion, in motivation. And they were the fastest runners in the world.

Puttnam had left America after making *Midnight Express* – a shattering exposure of human nature at its most bestial – with a sour taste in his mouth. It was a cynical film, he says, and its instant triumph at the box-office and with the critics only disillusioned him. The acclaim he now enjoyed as Britain's most successful film-maker brought him little joy. He had a string of films behind him already – the award-winning *The Duellists*,

Bugsy Malone, That'll Be the Day, Brother, Can You Spare a Dime? and others. But the taste of success was never as sweet as he had imagined it would be.

He was ready now to make a film that was different. 'We live in such an expedient society,' he says, using again the word that sums up for him much of what is wrong with our world today. 'I have felt that for a long time. I became more and more interested in people who choose not to be expedient, and it seemed that sport could be a wonderful metaphor, a more accessible metaphor than religion in, for instance, Robert Bolt's *A Man for All Seasons.*'

He looked around for the kind of script-writer whose work would reflect the spirit of the idea he had in mind, and he hit at last upon Colin Welland, the actor who had starred in *Z Cars* and *Kes* before developing into an author and playwright as well. Welland had written the original screenplay of the film *Yanks*, and a succession of award-winning television plays such as *Roll On Four O'Clock*, *Leeds United*, *Kisses at Fifty* and *Your Man from Six Counties*.

'There is something heroic about Colin Welland's writing,' says David Puttnam. 'It occasionally goes over the top, but it is marvellous, unembarrassed, heroic writing. And that is what we needed. I gave him the material.'

Colin Welland went wading into the research with enthusiasm, poring for months over diaries and books and newspaper cuttings and papers in order to get inside the skin of Eric Liddell.

'I got to know Eric Liddell,' he says, 'essentially by reading about him a great deal and talking about him to people who had known him; but in particular I was hugely helped by a young man who had never actually met him – he's far too young – but has more or less modelled his life on him.'

The man who was so helpful to Colin Welland in his search for Eric Liddell was John Keddie, a thirty-four-year-old London Scot, born and brought up in Edinburgh. Keddie was an outstanding member of Edinburgh Southern Harriers in the 1960s; he won the Scottish Junior Triple Jump championship and was runner-up in the 400 metres. At the age of nineteen, when he was competing on the senior athletics circuit, his brother, now a minister in the USA, sent him a booklet about

Liddell 'to encourage me to become more involved in spiritual things and get a better balance in my life'. John Keddie was so impressed by the Liddell story that he not only joined an evangelical Christian group but refused to take part in the Sunday meetings of the Scottish Amateur Athletics League.

Had that ruined his athletics career? 'No, I don't think I was ever going to be the greatest, but I was one of the key runners then, and when another chap and I refused to run I think our club persuaded the League to change to Saturday meetings. But it was Liddell's example that gave me the courage to stand my ground. Once I had done it I was able to take a much more balanced view of running. It ceased to be the be-all and end-all of my life. I became a really committed Christian and a keen supporter of Sunday observance. I even worked for the Lord's Day Observance Society for some years as an accountant. I made a complete survey of Liddell's life and published it in the *Athletics Weekly*. That's why I was able to help Colin Welland with details. I don't know that I would go as far as to say that I modelled my life on Eric Liddell's, but he certainly had a powerful influence in redirecting my life.'

John Keddie was able to tell Colin Welland a great deal about Liddell, about how he preached, how he expressed himself, and the things he wouldn't say as well as the things he did:

'For instance,' says Welland, 'John Keddie told me that Eric would never say "Good luck!" – he didn't believe in chance, he believed in Providence. Now, I would almost certainly have had Eric saying "Good luck!" in the pre-race sequences, when he went around shaking hands with the other contestants and wishing them well. I can't remember what I have him saying – "All the best", or something like that, but certainly not "Good luck!" '

Welland found Liddell a very appealing character – 'All the more so when I went to meet his sister in Edinburgh, and people like the lady who had been his great schoolgirl fan, Mrs Elsa Watson. What came through was a picture of someone very cheery, full of fun and tricks, very chirpy, not at all sanctimonious. I never got the impression at any time of "wetness". Anyone who could stand up to the athletics establishment as he did isn't wet. Actually, Eric put me rather in mind of someone like Lord Soper, the Methodist preacher, whom I've met – very straight, very vigorous, never prepared to compromise on principles. Lord Soper is one of the most vigorous and exciting men I've ever met, and – well, let's put it like this – if Soper could have run the 400 metres, he would be Eric Liddell; but a much more aggressive Eric Liddell, I think.

'I'm sure there are still men like Liddell around, but probably not in sport. Top sportsmen aren't usually like that. They have their principles up to a point, but there is also this compelling urgency to make their success before they pass their peak, and so they swallow their principles and go off to compete in South Africa, or in Moscow, or wherever. It's very rare to find anyone who would give up what Liddell did, just for the sake of a principle.'

But Eric Liddell also provided problems for the script-writer. Drama thrives on inner conflict, on family dissension, last-minute surprises: Liddell's decision not to run on a Sunday had none of these. So Welland wrote some disapproval into the part of Eric's sister, Jenny; he compressed the Olympic timetable and had Liddell discovering only on his way to Paris that the heats of the 100 metres were to be on a Sunday; he introduced Jenny to Eric's brother Rob as spectators in Paris, when they were both actually in China at the time, he invented a race between Liddell and Abrahams, the race which actually would have taken place if Abrahams had not developed a septic throat at the AAA Championships at Stamford Bridge in 1923. Another problem arose when Douglas Lowe, winner of the 800 metres for Great Britain in the 1924 Olympics, declined to co-operate with the film-makers: Welland had to invent a fictitious character instead, a dilettante aristocrat who emerged from his pen as a hurdler, not an 800 metres man. This was 'Lord Linsey' in the film, fictitious winner of the silver medal in the 400 metres hurdles.

But it was only in the details of the story that the film-makers allowed themselves the luxury of improving on history. The personalities of the two men were sacrosanct; they were to be represented exactly as research showed them to have been. David Puttnam watched the research developing, with mounting fascination.

'Liddell and Abrahams became more and more interesting because it became more and more clear that here was the chance to do a film about the two "me's". Abrahams is the "me" as I am: rather . . . *driven*. And Liddell is the man I would like to be and try to pretend that I am.

'They represent two attitudes to victory. Abrahams gets little out of winning; he ends up feeling sick. The winning wasn't worth the effort. Liddell does it out of a sense of love; running for him is its own *raison d'être*.'

But his friends were sceptical of what he was trying to do. No contemporary audience would be able to understand anyone refusing to run for Liddell's reason, they said. Puttnam was rattled. He still believed it would work, but he found it impossible to explain to anybody why he thought so. In the end, after the casting, he realized the missing factor was simply the performance of the actor in the part. He would either carry the conviction of the role, or he would not. When he saw Ian Charleson in the role he knew he had the man he needed.

Ian Charleson is a young Scottish actor who was born and brought up in Edinburgh, where he attended the Royal High School and, by a happy coincidence, Edinburgh University. He studied architecture there to begin with, and then, when he found himself developing an interest in acting, switched to an MA degree. After he graduated from Edinburgh he won a place at the London Academy of Music and Dramatic Art. Thereafter he joined the Young Vic, and played Guildenstern in Tom Stoppard's *Rosencrantz and Guildenstern Are Dead*. He then played Hamlet with the Royal Cambridge Theatre's production, and followed this with a triumphant West End début, playing a Glasgow lout in *Otherwise Engaged*.

Like David Puttnam and Colin Welland, Ian Charleson also spent long hours trying to understand Eric Liddell, and come to grips with the mystery of his simple faith.

'It was an incredible faith,' says Charleson. 'I think it took precedence over everything – even over himself. In order to understand him, I read the Bible from beginning to end. I had to find something in the Christian faith that I could feel with him. And I found lots in it that is very true for anybody. There is some incredible wisdom in the Bible.

'When you are acting a part you have to take on as much of the character as you can. You have to find elements in yourself which you can use, so that you can be real to yourself. I am a fairly easy-going person as a rule. I just used my nice side for the part and tried to suppress my baser instincts. I came across as just that: someone who is not a victim of his base instincts. Liddell was like that.'

Charleson found his own personality changing for a time as he drew to the surface these elements that brought him close to Liddell: 'What I admired about him was his serenity. My whole personality changed during the time I was doing the part. I became very slow and laconic.'

The problem of making the simple goodness of Liddell's character interesting exercised him greatly. 'It was a great worry. What I was terrified of was playing a real goody-goody, the kind of person you want to punch because he is so bloody holy. But I discovered that he wasn't like that. He *is* interesting. It's this faith of his again. Anyone who can believe that strongly in something and not push it as a dogma, and not use it as a crutch for his life, has got to be interesting.

'The way I see it, he never pushed his faith down anyone's throat. When he spoke, he spoke rather quietly. He just talked about real things – about himself and his faith and what he did that morning.'

Colin Welland, the script-writer, is not one to romanticize about the effect of the Liddell story, either on himself or, through the film, on the public. He describes himself as 'an agnostic leaning towards belief', or what Brendan Behan called a 'daylight atheist'. He is not leaning either more or less towards belief since writing the Liddell script. That kind of thing, he says, cannot come second-hand: 'It happens personally, you can't wish it on yourself.' Nor does he accept Liddell's priorities.

'For instance, I don't agree with his anti-drink stance, and I don't think Sunday is sacrosanct. I'm a director of Fulham Rugby League Club and we're having bother with local people and the Lord's Day Observance Society over Sunday games and whether we can play music over the loudspeakers or just in the club. All right, Sunday's a day of rest, but rest is relaxation and people ought to be able to enjoy their relaxation in their own way. But Sunday mattered to Liddell and he stood by what he believed in. I understood that. I understood a man of conscience.

'I think I would have liked Liddell, as I like Donald Soper. I enjoyed writing the film very much, and I think the public will like it. It's an adventure story with heroes, and a real cliff-hanging situation. Films like that *are* finding an audience these days – *Breaking Away*, for instance, and *Rocky*. But I don't think *Chariots of Fire* is going to influence people's lives or morals. I have never contributed to the idea that films and plays have any lasting effect on people. They're entertainment. And I'm completely cynical about the entertainment business. If *Chariots of Fire* is a hit there'll be a spate of films about high-principled sportsmen. If there was a box-office hit about public hanging they'd make a spate of films about that, too.'

But the film *is* different, says Welland, with its drawing together of sport and sociology, conflict and personality. Getting to know Eric Liddell through it did not influence him, or change him, or do any of the things a journalist likes to put into someone's mouth to round off a good story. 'But I'll never forget that film,' he says.

Charleson says he got a lot out of playing the part of Liddell. 'I learned a lot from the man. That may sound corny, but it's true. You can't read the Bible with the kind of care I did without learning something yourself. I don't know if I believe in a supreme God the way Eric did, but it makes a lot of sense. For instance, there's a bit in the Bible that really impressed me – all about it not being that which goes into a man that defiles him, but that which goes out. That really made me think. Something like that strikes a chord in me because I know it's true.

'It's not too fanciful to say you can learn a lot from a man like Eric Liddell. But whether I can ever live like him is very doubtful.'

For David Puttnam it will always be a very special film: 'I love it because it's been like a hot shower. I came out of America pretty knocked about. I didn't enjoy *Midnight Express*. We just made it because we wanted to prove to the Americans that we were better at making films than them. When a film you are really cynical about is successful, it shakes you.

'And so when I got back to England at first I wasn't sure if I wanted to be in the film industry any longer. I felt the weight of this extraordinarily expedient career on me. So I turned round and made a totally inexpedient film. It was the most unlikely of stories, after all. So for me it has been a very cathartic film. It has made me feel clean again.'

He wonders sometimes if this film is not a little too early to win back a public so disillusioned with the film industry that it shuns the cinema now. 'All of us in the media are enormously influenced by a small coterie of cynical people. The amount of time that I spend among ordinary people, just ordinary people, is very small. There is an audience out there that we in the media have lost. I hope the film is not just a fraction too early. My real concern – and it's a very difficult one to deal with – is that the audience which is going to love this picture may be the one that has given up on the cinema.'

But the change is coming, he believes. The public is aching for heroism again, and sooner or later the film industry will realize it. At the moment, he says, the film industry is conspiring to create its own death.

The period of making *Chariots of Fire* in his later thirties coincided for Puttnam, strangely or not so strangely, with a reassessment of his own religious beliefs. 'Having survived the 1960s and 1970s, I am now absolutely convinced that we are not able to live without an injection of something additional in our lives. Four years ago I couldn't have said that. I believe absolutely in God, and during the time I have been working on this film all of these beliefs happened to solidify. Yes, Liddell was part of that, I suppose, as other things were too.

'I sometimes wonder: What made me suddenly find the paragraph in that book when I had been reading that kind of thing for years without noticing Liddell? Why, at the time of life when I had enough clout to put on a film like that, should I suddenly find the book?'

David Puttnam apologizes for being fanciful, but, however diffidently, he cannot stop talking about the 'specialness' of the Liddell film. In Hugh Hudson they had come upon an unknown director with no major film to his credit, who had revealed an amazingly sensitive feel for what Puttnam was trying to do. 'There is no director in the world who could have done it as he did it,' he said. The editor, Terry Rawlings, one of the most down-to-earth of a hard-bitten breed, had become unprecedentedly caught up with the film and its story. Even the cameraman had become excited. That is David Puttnam's story, anyway. The emotion in *Midnight Express*, he says, was 'crafted into it' by detached professionals, who calculated the impact of every scene. In *Chariots*, however, 'the emotion comes from within.'

Perhaps it wouldn't be too fanciful, either, to suppose that the *sancta simplicitas* – the sacred simplicity – of a man like Eric Liddell will continue to reverberate gently down the years, and affect all sorts of unlikely people. The secret of that charisma of his, still touching people from 1920s schoolgirl to 1980s filmmaker, has to be his faith – though that may be too simple an answer for our times. It has to be something to do with the resources he tapped when his head jerked back in a race and he ran blind; something to do with the spiritual source he surrendered to when the fighting was over. Whatever his secret, it will be found there where the joy and the pain and the love were greatest.

If that is too simple an answer for an age that tends to be more comfortable with the unresolved paradox of a life that comprehends both drive and serenity, will to achieve and grace to give in, ordinariness and charisma – then it's probably a comment on us. For in the end there is really no paradox, no enigma about Eric Liddell's life: wasn't it Burns who said, for his own purposes, that a simple man is 'a problem that puzzles the devil'?